*I dedicate this book to my wonderful parents,
Brian and Mandy Schlachter (Mama and Papa
hippo), who have sacrificed so much to put me
in the position that I am today.*

1

Let's do Something Different.

Preface

What started out as me blogging about my various aquatic and land based ultra-distance endeavours on my Zimhippo blog has expanded into a 10-year adventure that has challenged and changed my life immeasurably. This book is about one man's journey to making that change. It is by no means autobiography; the parts of my life that I have shared in this book are there mainly to give context. It is also not a manual on how to undertake endurance events but is my own humble experience that I hope will provide you with an insight into the wonderful world of sport and inspire you to take up your own journey,

This is My Hippo Aquatic oath.

A question to start you off.

Why is it that hippos, being the size that they are and having lungs the size they do, can remain submerged for such a long time?

Answer at the end.

Table of contents

Chapter 1 – How it all began

In 2007, I had been living in London for ten years, and to put it frankly, I was in a rut that was fast threatening to become a sinkhole. I had fallen into a bad routine of working and partying and I was on a fast train to nowhere. I spent weekends and evenings living it up in the bars and clubs of the capital. After leaving the country of my birth, I had done a fair amount of travelling and I'd had some great experiences along the way. But it was the rigours of life that had got me to this point. Leaving my home and starting a life from nothing was hard to do, particularly having to leave my loving family in Zimbabwe, and not being able to see my parents when I wanted, but only on fleeting visits once every two years. I changed my career multiple times in that eleven years. The knocks and lessons learnt had been hard. In fact, there were often moments that I looked back at my life and allowed my mind to wander to thoughts of WHAT IF! My self-esteem was at an all-time low, and I had become a Zim Hippo – from Zimbabwe, good at wallowing in water and HEAVY. I drank and smoked too much, and due to an eleven-year hiatus from any form exercise which had always been an integral part of my upbringing, I was the heaviest I had ever been in my life. I had the bases covered - I had a roof over my head, and a job that was really not inspiring me. I was a lot more fortunate than many that I knew who had had their lives ripped apart by choosing to make Africa their home. The funny thing about being in a rut is that although I had noticed it, I did not seem to have the motivation or the drive to get out of it. My life routine had become mundane. Wake up, go to work, sit at a desk all day, get home, collapse on the sofa and while away the evenings – into the wee hours of the morning – mindlessly staring at whatever rubbish was on TV. The "conquer all" attitude of my late teens and early twenties had all but vanished.

I was not alone in this realisation. My brother Spencer had also noticed it and whilst he was travelling down to a sailing regatta in Italy with a long standing friend, Nick Jones, (he had known my brother and I almost our whole lives) they discussed my predicament, trying to figure out how they could get me out of it. It must have been a long journey! But it seems that their musings were not in vain.

It all began with a simple question - my brother the perpetrator, and I the idle one on the couch, watching whatever flickering images were in front of me, one murky winter's evening. I was in my usual routine and my comfort zone - get home, change into my fat pants and slump onto the sofa for the night. Tonight would be different.

The phone sang out and I answered it. My brother was on the other end and after the usual pleasantries, he quickly got to the point. The ensuing conversation went a bit like this.

Him: "How about we do something different next summer?'

Me; "Okay, I'll bite, what are you thinking about?"

"How about we go and swim the English Channel next summer?"

Silence. Then with incredulity in my voice; "What drugs have you been on?! That is possibly the stupidest thing I have ever heard. Do you not know they have planes and boats and the like to get us to France?"

He did at least try his best to convince me, but at the time, and possibly quite justifiably so, I really did think it was a very stupid idea and the subject was dropped - for a few months.

But from that night, it got me thinking. My sedentary lifestyle was taking its toll; having gained so much weight, the inevitable niggles had started to appear, one of them being back problems from carrying too much Hippo around. Up till that point, during my time in London I had tried to get back into sport a couple of times, but each time I was totally put off by the process. I had previously attempted to join the local rowing group as my wife at the time, Rachelle, and I had both rowed when we were younger. We thought it would be a grand idea to get back into it again. Well, the fitness test that I was put through just to be able to qualify for the privilege of POSSIBLY becoming a member nearly killed me. Even if we had have been granted membership, we would then have had to compete for a position on one of the boats. To me this was total madness! I had only ever done my sport for fun and then progressed from there; all this competition just to be able to exercise really put me off the whole affair as the FUN had been totally removed from the whole thing. I inevitably gave up on that idea.

Having failed to get back into rowing, my next opportunity to become involved in sport again came while I was living in the Docklands area of London. On one of the docks they had a small sailing club and while strolling past, I noticed a sign up mentioning that they were looking for someone to assist in teaching people to sail. The boats were small mirror boats so nothing I could not handle, having sailed boats from 10 feet to 110 feet. I phoned and went for an interview and they were very impressed with my sailing experience, but it all fell apart when I was asked what qualifications I had. I really had no paper qualifications, just a wealth of experience. Being the law-abiding modern world, all they were interested in is a piece of paper that said I could sail. Passion and experience it seemed counted for nothing in this weird world. It made me furious! That and the issue that people did not seem to do sport for fun anymore put me back on my trajectory to nowhere for the next 3 – 4 years.

I knew though that my back problems were not going to go away. A procession of trips to chiropractors, osteopaths and physiotherapists in the last few years had all helped in their own little way, but nothing had really resolved the problem, and my scoliosis just seemed to add to it all. I joined the local gym and try as I may, I just could not get into a routine with it. The sofa was much more comfortable.

But to swim to France?! That's just stupid.

Chapter 2: The years of trying

Before I go on, this journey will not be complete without a brief outline of what brought me to where I am.

Sport for me has never been something I have strived to do. It has taken on various guises throughout my life, but I have always been in it for fun, without the desire or the ability to take it to the next level. Despite these odds, I have somehow done fairly well throughout my life.

A good place to start is the beginning. I was born in Zimbabwe, which not only has the ideal climate for outdoor sports, but is arguably the best climate in the world. From a very young age, I was around sport of one type or another. My father was an exceptional horseman who represented his country at Polocrosse - a cross between Polo and Lacrosse. My mother also excelled at swimming at school. With their dream to have their own stables and horses, it was inevitable that horses were part of my life from a very young age. We became involved in the little known sport of Sulky racing - a sport popular in America and in Europe, where a small trap/carriage is harnessed to a horse, and raced around a sand track measuring 1km or 1 mile, with the aim to keep the horse at a trot. If your horse does break into a canter, you are penalised. Therefore, most weekends and weekday mornings were spent training the horses for the track. The early hours and time put in during the week before my mother and father disappeared off to earn a living were reflected at race meets on the weekends. Sadly, the sport of Sulky racing collapsed in my early years, leaving us with a string of horses and nothing to do with them, so we started the arduous task of cross training them into dressage and show jumping. As we had our own horses, it was only natural that riding was a big part of my life. Many long hours were spent bouncing around on my steed until I finally mastered the art of trotting, cantering, jumping and dressage, while my riding teacher set all sorts of weird and wonderful challenges to hone my balance on a horse.

My years at junior school were a little different in that most kids got to take their gym kit and books to school - I got to take my horse with me for the semesters! I was a boarder at a small school called Dudley Hall, in the Norton area in Zimbabwe, a great little school catering predominantly for children of the farming communities. My Mother had gone there in her earlier years. Boarding meant we were at school for the entire term, only let out every 4th weekend on an exeat weekend where we were allowed to go home for a few days. Well, having my horse with me was a lot better than her staying at home and only being able to ride her on exeat weekends! Mhanyapisa was her name, which translates to Run Hot from the local vernacular. I entered gymkhanas and the like, but horse-riding was only a small part of my extra-curricular activities, as I was obligated to take part in other sports. The crisp dry winter was spent doing athletics and, as I grew older, rugby. The long hot summer was perfect for wallowing around one pool or another, training to be a swimmer. It was soon apparent that I was not really that good at anything that required speed on land, but what also became noticeable was the ability to sustain exercise for longer periods - so I ran – yes ran, in the longer distances. Being a boarder at school, we were generally up with the sparrows and out doing something, either on land, or in the pool or lakes. Or, when at home, in the horse swimming pool, as you do. During the school holidays, we used to have to hack (long rides in the countryside to exercise our horses) a fair bit. We sometimes would ride them all the way to the local lake where we would meet up with the rest of the family for lunch and a swim – with the horses – before riding them back home. There was plenty of fun stuff to keep us busy.

By this time, I was becoming pretty adept in the saddle. Having started with dressage, I moved into show jumping, so it became all about riding or breaking horses. One day, we adopted a horse from the trotting years, which had to be broken and then trained up for show jumping. He was a brute of a horse at 17.2 hands (or 1.74 metres at his shoulder), not very pretty, but bold as they come when it came to jumping. When we rode, it was not a question of my ability as a jumper, but more my ability to hold on, as this animal pretty much threw itself headlong at anything you pointed him at – apart from a water jump, of course.

While I was dallying with horses, our next-door neighbour invited my brother Spencer to attend the local sailing school, as someone had pulled out at the last minute. This was a great thing because as we were both involved in horse-riding, this gave my brother an opportunity to enter into something totally different - and so for a few years he was the sailor and I was the horse-rider. He took to it exceptionally well and was soon moving up the ranks, winning regional and then national sailing events and even qualifying for international events. While I was very good at staying on a horse, school terms were still spent doing my swimming and rugby. I learnt pretty young that I would never be good at athletics but I was proving pretty swift in the pool.

I was about twelve when I was on the receiving end of a kick to the head by one of our resident horses. It left me blind in one eye, and it required pretty major surgery to at least put my eye back in my head. I'll spare you the gory details, but fortunately I only have the dents in my skull to remember it by, as my full vision fortunately returned three years later. As I'm sure you can appreciate, my love for horses took a pretty sharp downturn, and even my swimming was brought to an abrupt halt as I was not allowed in the pool while my eye healed. My interest in sport took a huge blow. My brother was however doing quite well in his sailing, so holidays and weekends were now spent following him around. I'm sure I don't need to tell you that sitting on the shores watching someone sailing in the distance is by no means a great spectator sport, and boredom overtook me! Before long I found myself on a friend's boat, trying this drifting-around-a-lake malarkey for myself. It stuck, and before we knew it, both my brother and I were in the sailing world. Spencer became national champion and then moved onto international events, representing his country three times. It took me some time to get to grips with floating around in a small boat such as the Optimist - this is a vessel usually used for beginner sailors, and definitely more suited to the leaner build of person... of which I definitely was not! It did make my parents' life a bit easier with us both sailing though, as they did not have to split their time between two sons with vastly differing interests.

When Spencer came of age, he was no longer allowed to sail Optimists, as the age cut-off was 15. He decided to move on to the Enterprise, and as this was a two-man boat, he needed a crew. I was pretty rubbish in the Optimist, being rather rotund, and my brother was an amazing tactician on the water – he clearly needed a bit of ballast for his new venture in this new type of boat, so at a very young age, I followed him in his pursuit and became his crew. With his ability to read the waters and winds, and me with my ability to add ballast and defy all odds, we became a successful sibling team (I say defying the odds as it was very unusual for siblings to sail together successfully). We both knew our places and we were good at what we did - above all we trusted each other. Before long, we had reached the top of the national rankings and were selected to go international. We had to turn it down, as I was just thirteen years old.

When I started secondary school, I had to do school sports, so I signed up for rugby. The other options were hockey, cricket, squash and tennis, but I had discovered that my hand-eye coordination was pretty diabolical, possibly due to the aforementioned kicking I had taken from a horse. Yes, you guessed it -I was in the scrum, and played flank or eighth man. We were also urged to take on something else, and I chose rowing as a third sport as it was compulsory to do athletics. I wasn't as good on the track, but I could throw things quite far and also do a bit of pole-vault. As I was still boarding at school, we often used to wake up early and hit the fields or pool for a bit of training of some sort. So, weekends were a bit of a juggling act, what with swimming galas, sailing or rugby, and the odd weekend of rowing thrown in. In swimming, I was selected for a school trip to Mauritius and La Reunion for an international meet. My poor parents spent about eight years of their life when at least one of their children was swanning off on some international meet or another - not to mention ferrying us around the countryside to various matches, athletics meets, galas or regattas! Over and above all this, they also had to raise the funds to send us there. They have my utmost admiration and respect.

The years went by quickly, and it was soon time for my brother to end his schooling and head to university. This left me at a bit of a loss as I now did not have a helm (boat driver) to sail with. I spent a few months crewing with other people until I found a helm that I really worked well with. We got to the top of the national league again, becoming national champions, and we were selected to represent our country at the world championships in Mumbai, where I was the youngest crew at fifteen years of age. My time in Mumbai was my first off the continent of Africa - an experience which will forever stay in my mind. Unfortunately, when we returned, my helm then moved onto other things, but I found another and was again selected for the world championships, this time in Durban in South Africa. With all these selections, my sport required more and more of my time, training and keeping at the top of my game. But I was a teenager and I had other things which were slowly drawing my focus, and this came in the form of the fairer sex. It turned out that in the sailing world, there were a few young ladies with an interest in horse-riding!

As fate would have it, we still had our horses, which I grant you, I had pretty much ignored for the last two to three years, apart from having to walk past them to go and see my grandmother. My parents in the meantime had opened a livery stable which was now home to several horses, including ours. Strangely, my interest in horses was magically rekindled, and I even ended up doing a bit of teaching. These ladies fell in love with the sport, purchased their own horses and kept them at my parents' place, and in no time, the livery stable was filled to capacity. Several became proficient enough to take their horse-riding abilities to the next level, into show jumping and doing dressage. I, in turn, got back into competing in the saddle and was more a dressage specialist than a showjumper, but we did still have the brute of a horse, Longshanks, so I carried on with both. However, the horse-riding world failed to hold my interest, as the horses I competed with were not thoroughbreds, but had been retrained from our Sulky racing days into these areas. It was not really the done thing to bring a non-thoroughbred horse to a dressage or show jumping event and then win it! The whole environment did not work with me, although I did enjoy the jumping. It turns out that Longshanks was a great jumper.

One day some friends of mine were taking part in a triathlon. They were doing it as a team, so they needed a swimmer. This was to be the start of a drift into the weird world of triathlons for me. This was pretty much a natural progression in a way, as I was already a decent swimmer, taking part in regional galas and selected for international trials. There was only one small problem - the training for this not only took place at another school to the one I was boarding at, but also started at 4.30am. Now, I may be a morning person, but there was no way I was waking up at 3.30am to cycle six miles in the dark to do two hours of training, then cycle back for a full day of lectures. I was given the option of training on my own, and I did try this out, but training on your own is not quite the same. Also, not being able to gauge the competition you are up against is also challenging – in effect, the fun was taken out of my swimming. So, although I did do well at school level in the pool, I did not quite make it on to the national level, even though I could compete fairly strongly, specifically as a butterfly specialist. Fortunately though, being good swimmer was a good thing in triathlons. I started out doing mostly team events. The cycling and the running were not that important to me as I was there to do the swim leg. However, as I was taking part already, why not do the whole event on my own? For this I needed equipment in the form of a bicycle so I got rid of some of my sailing kit and my horse to fund this, and off I went. I began taking part in triathlons on a national level, travelling around the country and regionally competing. The only issue was that I was a terrible runner! I was never destined to get very far in this game. I would happily hold my own in the water and on the bike, but my running let me down terribly, so I only ever achieved a third in the All-Africa games. I carried on with triathlons for a few years, branching out into road racing, and got more involved with that. But none of them really held my attention for that long, probably because I actually had to do some training. Because I lived slightly out of town, I trained on my own, apart from the weekends, when I had the opportunity to meet with others. When you are a teenager, training alone seems to take the fun out of things.

Many moons ago in my triathlon days

While I was being your typical teenager, my parents were working hard to provide the wherewithal that I needed to keep up with my sporting adventures. It was at about this time that a chance meeting with an Australian at a plant convention in South Africa caused my parents' direction in life to change. Our friend was not only in South Africa for the plant convention, but also to give a seminar in personal development, a four-day course that effectively enables a person to access more of their mental capability. My parents were given an invitation to attend the course in South Africa and, although sceptical, they came back pretty blown away - blown away enough to throw all their savings into organising these seminars in Zimbabwe. To say they were a success is an understatement, as we ran the biggest seminars this guy had ever run. There was nothing like it in the country, and we did quite a few of them. Not only did the lecturer get to run his biggest seminars, but he also got to explore and experience some of the best Safari areas in the world at the same time. As these seminars were so well subscribed, I was asked to attend one of them. It was an intense four days, but it was a key point in my life that gave me the tools and techniques for getting through some of the toughest challenges that lay ahead of me.

My last few years in Africa were spent in college with the aim of having some qualifications behind me before I embarked on my next adventure to go and see the world. They were very happy times, spent in the African sun, but many amazing adventures awaited me. I left with a little money and a dream of working on super-yachts, and really, much to my mother's horror, with no idea of how exactly to achieve it. Through a bit of luck, a few contacts and hard work, I spent a year doing exactly that in the Mediterranean, but by the time it came to go home, my home country was in a very different place. I made my home in London, and there began effectively a twelve-year break from any form of exercise, sport and competition.

Chapter 3: The Journey begins

Back to 2007, when my brother decided to weigh in and take a punt at trying to get me fit again. I was still convinced his suggestion was a bit mad.

But with my trajectory still firmly set to "going nowhere", my health was beginning to suffer. I was finding it harder and harder to do anything that required me to bend down or carry anything. Unfortunately, my job required me to be crawling under and behind desks and server room racks, which aggravated my back even more. I have an interesting frame, with a very long torso and short stubby legs. With that long torso, comes a case of very minor scoliosis. While on the hunt again for a fix, a good friend put me in touch with their trusted physiotherapist. It took only one meeting with him to make me think - and what he said made a LOT of sense to me.

After an initial examination and some sports massage, he asked me, "What supports what in your body? Does the skeleton support the muscles or do the muscles support the skeleton?"

I did not know the answer to this question, so he carried on. "They both work symbiotically. Each one supports the other and more importantly, both need to be maintained. With the scoliosis you have, you can spend the rest of your life getting your back manipulated but no matter what happens, the muscles will always pull it out of place again. That is currently how they have been trained. All you need to do is pick up something in an odd way, and you'll be back."

This made a huge amount of sense to me, having been put in a way that I could get my head around. His advice was simple: "Go and get your back put into place (manipulated) and once that is done, get fit – QUICKLY."

The first part was easy; another trip to the chiropractor and a substantial lightening of my wallet would easily have this remedied. The second was a bit more of a challenge and left me with a big question... How do you take an obese unfit smoker, who has not done any exercise in many years. with the attention span of a gnat – and get fit 'QUICKLY'?

I needed a challenge, not just your average challenge as I had proved to myself many times when I was young that I can probably get through most things on a wing and a prayer. What I needed was something big, something that would force me to get up off the sofa and train.

I started by trying to increase my time in the gym with this dilemma in mind. As some people might know, I am not really a gym sort of person and although I did make an effort to get into the gym mentality, I really was not very enthusiastic about pumping iron or doing circuits; they both bored me to death. It all seemed entirely pointless. Often when I was at the gym doing circuits, I overlooked the pool and I spent my time watching the swimmers doing their lengths instead. So much so, that one day, instead of heading to the gym, I dug out my ten year old swimming costume (which now barely covered the vastness of my body) and a pair of old goggles that I used to use when I last raced in a pool, and followed the smell of chlorine. I must have been a sight, squeezed into my "budgie smugglers", sporting a pair of goggles that now leaked due to the ravages of time on the gel seal.

I decided to at least see what I was capable of in the pool, apart from emptying it when I dived in. That was the first problem; living in the first world with health and safety being what it is, I very quickly found out that diving into an indoor pool in the First World is not really the done thing. At least I gave the lifeguards something to do, as they were very quick in rushing over to chastise me for infringement of the rules. After learning the error of my ways, I eased myself into the tepid warm – actually HOT water. Could I still swim? Despite my now very large frame, I could still get to the end of the pool and back. It felt quite natural in fact! My next test surprised me even more. Many moons previously, I had loved the sense of being underwater and I would spend many hours either sitting on the bottom of a pool holding my breath, held down by a few bricks (still here Mom!) or alternatively, swimming lengths underwater. It was a bit of a competition between us when we were youngsters, with my record being just over 115 metres (m). So when I managed just over three lengths of a 25m (about 85m), I was pretty impressed with myself. The surprise was short lived - my second disciplinary infringement had just taken place! The lifeguards were once again galvanised into action, and they let me know that swimming lengths underwater was not the done thing either! Did I not know I could die due to shallow water blackout?! Was that even a thing? My first time back in the pool after about twelve years was going well - barely ten minutes in, and I had already found myself on the wrong side of the law with not one, but two things you are NOT allowed to do in a public pool.

Oh well! I got down to doing a few base tests that hopefully would not end in another infringement to see what I was capable of. Get in, and over 100m, 200m, 300m, do a timed easy and a timed fast pace and gauge where exactly I was with this swimming. Mmmm. Lots of room for improvement! One area where there was not a lot of room though was my swimming trunks; a better fitting speedo and a new set of non-leaking goggles were required! With the bit between my teeth, I then set myself a task of swimming at least three times a week. I joined up with the Masters group and was in the slow lane to start off with, but over time, I worked my way up the lanes. It dawned on me that I was actually not too bad at this floating thing. Soon I was leading the fast lane. All this swimming was definitely making a difference but, without a goal, my motivation was still AWOL. I began to find that I *looked forward* to the end of my sessions after ploughing my way through between 2.5 and 3.5 kilometres. I could not wait to get out and back to my comfort zone. There was no doubt that I did enjoy this swimming way more than the gym, but I was still faced with the question - how can I up the ante and keep my focus up? I was at a loss as to how to address my physiotherapist's advice to get fit QUICKLY.

While I was swimming fairly regularly and making good progress at getting fitter, in the midst of a swim set one night, and with my dilemma at the very front of my consciousness, my brother's attempt to get me off the sofa came drifting to the fore. As soon as I got home, I switched on my laptop and began looking up this Channel swimming madness on the internet with a huge dose of scepticism. Madness! I started with the statistics about how few people had done it. This swim was the 'biggest swim in the world', with a diabolical success rate. The fact that you might have to wait three to four weeks just to get out there and then have to contend with tides, the cold, saltwater, jellyfish… Eish. This really did not sound like something I wanted, or ever believed I could do. I was just an average guy with not a hell of a lot of drive, and here I was looking at something that for most had been a lifelong dream, and for me was for the realms of the extraordinary people who trained for years to do something like this. It really did not sound like me. But, 'if successful, you will enter into a very elite group of people' – at that point in time, less than a thousand people had ever done it. It was, and still is, known as the Everest of swimming. Mt Everest itself had been summited by about four and a half thousand people at the time so to become part of this very elite group…well. This really did not sound like me. I was nothing special and to do what some people would consider as extraordinary was just not in my makeup. I would feel like an imposter, a charlatan.

I carried on at the gym and wallowed around the pool, becoming more and more depressed at my lack of focus to keep up the training with any sort of energy. It's true, I did enjoy the outing three times a week and was happy that I was now leading the fast lane at the Masters class and holding my own very comfortably - but without a goal, I was just going through the motions and life carried on as normal. The seed was sown though and in my spare time I was researching English Channel swims. I found a few blogs and saw the eye-watering effort that people put into it. Some of the distances swum per week were probably more than I did in my car! This really was not something I would be able to do. But still I looked, still I read, and still I kept looking for a challenge. There had to be something to keep me focused, as I knew I would not succeed otherwise. I was just coasting along and while the gym did help my back, it was still giving me grief.

Chapter 4: Why Swimming?

After ten years of inactivity, why did I ultimately get back into swimming? Apart from what you have just read, I had many opportunities over my life to go in various directions. Horse-riding had always been a favourite of mine, as had sailing. Although I loved and did fairly well at both sports, they required a lot of time and a lot of money – especially in the United Kingdom. I once heard in conversation, "How do you make a small fortune by owning horses? You start off with a large fortune!" Having spent my formative years around horses in Africa, I can honestly vouch that this is pretty much true, as it is an expensive past-time. Sailing is particularly time consuming and costly too. Having some experience of each, I knew that the test of a good sailor or horse-rider is – in part – down to the participant's ability. The rest is down to equipment. If you can afford the best, it can make a big difference.

As previously mentioned, I also tried venturing into rowing in the UK, but that had ended badly. There seemed to be no such thing as doing a sport for fun. I found the same with triathlons in the UK - you could spend substantial amounts of money and again, the atmosphere did not sit well with me with everyone being so competitive. It appeared to be more about who has the best equipment than raw ability.

Open water swimming on the other hand, appealed to me as a very purist sport, in that the equipment needed was minimal. Trunks, goggles and cap. Your ability could not be improved by gadgets and technology. Yes, there is a plethora of gadgets and training aids out there nowadays, but very few have made it into open water competitions. Therefore, it would be a cheaper sport to do - so I thought! That was until I started entering open water swims. There are many out there, from short 1500 metres (m) to 15 kilometres (km), ranging in price from about £20 to about £100, and when you start wanting to swim across oceans, channels or massive lakes, the costs rise exponentially. It is understandable as, for an average English Channel, you need to hire a boat for about twenty four hours, often longer when you take into account getting to the start and then back again. I began to realise there was a reason why at the time, only about a thousand people had ever crossed the English Channel. When all costs are added up over the years preceding a challenge like that, gym memberships, trips for training, hotel and accommodation, time off work (I mention this as specifically the Channel crossings are very weather dependent and you can fly across the world only to have inclement weather and not even get to swim), it runs into thousands of pounds. On that basis, you must be one hundred percent committed.

It was obvious to me that the English Channel is not a small challenge, and that it would require lots of sacrifices. For many it is a lifestyle change rather than something that you do for a few years. A hundred percent committed was not something that I considered myself ever being. I loved sport for sport and fun, but to put the time, effort and finances into something that had a very low success rate and potentially put someone as insignificant as me into a very elite club... I was really struggling with it. This was a reflection of my state of mind at the time. My self-worth and self-esteem were at an all-time low. I just did not realise how low.

I didn't think about all this when I started, but as I sit here and try and answer the question "Why Swimming", I realise there are many reasons, but that actually, enjoyment is pretty low on the list.

In a nutshell - why do I *love* swimming Open water with little more than a pair of trunks on? – the solitude. Why do I *hate* Open water swimming? The solitude! Sounds weird, but let's explore this.

With our lives being SO busy in the modern world, it is essential that we need to take time out. For many people this is very difficult when trying to juggle work, home, fitness, family, friends, colleagues, social engagements and the like. For me, swimming gives me time to disappear into my own little bubble; no one can bother me. I have no access to the outside world, no phone, internet, email, social media or distraction of any kind. I am totally alone with my thoughts and it may sound contradictory, but the time I spend in the water is very relaxing. I may be expending a lot of physical energy, but it is a time to focus on my mental state with zero interruptions. This is the same for any endurance-based sport and for that alone, I can understand the draw to spend so much time in the water, or on a bike, running, rowing, whatever. It is essential for everyone to get away from life for a while, whatever they use - some use meditation, yoga, gym, Pilates, others reading, needlework, sewing, baking etc.etc. They all give you the opportunity to switch off and in this day and age, it is essential to your mental wellbeing. Switching off has become more and more of a problem in the modern world, and for me, putting myself in a situation where I can't access a screen of any kind is crucial to my mental health. It is a time for reflection and a wonderful opportunity to explore and test and challenge my mental side and the limits that they impose.

So, it is not necessarily that I love swimming. I may love wallowing in it but, to be honest, training quickly becomes tedious for me and I try to keep my training stints pretty short. Crucially, I mix up my training a lot, even if I am just using the pool as I do not see the point of dedicating an entire day to swimming. Yes, it has to be done during your initial years as an open water endurance swimmer, purely for you to learn what your mind will do when you hit "the Wall". But once you have a few eight to twelve hour endurance events under your belt, and you have decided that this endurance malarkey is a lifestyle choice rather than a one-off challenge, then maintaining your fitness is more important than pushing out the really big distances.

Another very important reason that keeps me coming back to this sport is the amazing people I have met along the way. It's something I really love about swimming as an endurance sport. For the most part, people are incredibly supportive, very enthusiastic, totally uplifting and most importantly, not particularly competitive in the normal sense of the word. Do not get me wrong - open water endurance swimmers are some of the most determined people I have met and show true grit! I mention the lack of competitiveness as it is very difficult to gauge and chart your successes in relation to others. Every swim for every person is very different. Tides, weather, wind, water temperatures, air temperatures, swarms of jellyfish, nothing is ever the standard for ALL swims. The challenge does not become against another swimmer, but more a challenge against yourself and the elements. It is the reason why there are no WORLD records for the 10 km marathon event in the Olympics, as the venues differ from year to year. Sometimes it is in lakes, sometimes in the ocean, and possibly in the future, rivers may come into play - therefore every time it is different, unlike the pool which is man-made and a controlled environment. One thing man struggles to do is to control the elements. Long may that last!

In case you needed another reason to love endurance swimming – although this would be for any form of sport – for us it's also the amazing places you can find yourself going to to get your fix. Once you get into it, you can expand your challenges into races or you can stick to lakes, or explore the oceans. What is gaining popularity nowadays – for the extremely foolhardy – (yes, I am one of them), is ice swimming. While I have never done an ice mile with an organising body, I have swum though two winters without a wetsuit and have done the distance, at similar and lower temperatures that would qualify me. I just don't have a record of it, but I do have fond memories of learning how my body reacts to the cold. Yes, the poles of this planet, always revered as the most inhospitable places out there, are now being probed by more and more bioprene addicted swimmers. There is even an Ice Swimming Federation, where the holy grail is the Ice Mile – which is to swim a mile (1600m) in water below five degrees Celsius ($^\circ$C).

Ultra-distance or endurance swimming also has a great appeal to me because it is a niche, albeit fast-growing sport. Unlike the more mainstream sports like triathlon, cycling, running – and many others that are VERY popular and have thousands of competitors, endurance swimming is quite small and you get to meet many of the greats, and often end up swimming with them on a regular basis. In general, the people that you meet are truly amazing and some of the most inspirational people that I have ever met.

Other fringe benefits of swimming are the obvious fitness that results, an increase in lung capacity, never having to wear deodorant as you constantly smell like chlorine, itchy skin, and hair that looks like a ball of straw... Oh, those last few are the negatives!!

So, while my preferred way to do sport and get away from the world is to venture into the water, I truly believe that all my dabbling as a child in many different sports is what has gotten me to where I am now. There are studies out there now that are putting the idea forward that if you want to become a great athlete, it is not necessarily about starting that sport at a VERY young age and then it being *all* you do your entire life, but a more holistic approach. By this I mean trying out different sports along the way, as each sport or adventure will teach you vital lessons and hone different skills so that when you put them all together you effectively become a better athlete for it. This idea is embraced more and more, with other forms of training being adopted into the primary sport. For instance, in swimming, - practice, practice, practice will get you a long way, but mixing it with other things like Pilates will inevitably give you an advantage. When I ventured into this game over ten years ago, my attitude was that if I am going to swim to France I better get swimming, and that was the only form or exercise I did in my entire training. Over the years however, I have found Pilates a very good companion to make me a better swimmer.

Chapter 5: How to decide.

I am often in awe of people who know exactly what they want in their life from a very young age. Take my wife, the Slimhippo. She knew from a very young age that she wanted to be a veterinary surgeon. Her whole schooling had been geared towards gaining the relevant O and A levels to be granted a position at university to take on the arduous five-year plus degree to be able to care for furry things. It takes the uncertainty out of your path ahead, and you are comforted by the knowledge that you know what you need to do to get where you want to be, and you plan your life accordingly. Whilst I am in awe of my partner, she is pretty blown away by my attitude toward life. I had absolutely no idea what I wanted to do with my life when I left school. I started with agriculture for a while, thinking I could follow in my father's footsteps and become a commercial farmer in Africa. I then ended up becoming an electrician. I moved overseas, spent a year sailing on super yachts, then ended up in London. Clearly my qualifications as a farmer in London did not hold much water – not many thousand-acre commercial farms in London! There was also not a heck of a lot of competitive sailing going on nearby. As I had very little experience as an electrician, I needed a job so I began working as a postman, before drifting into car sales and information technology (IT) software design, then sliding into broadcast engineering. So, a colourful past. Whilst my wife's admiration lies in the fact that my approach imparts a fairly diverse set of abilities, I on the other hand admire the idea of knowing exactly what you want, with your whole life driven towards getting to that goal.

This seems to be the same for many (not all) open water and Channel swimmers and endurance athletes in general. They have a lifelong, or at least a very deep-seated desire to immerse themselves in their chosen endeavour for hours on end to achieve what for them is a long-held goal. Their lives are altered for months, and in many cases, years, to sharpen their skills and hopefully make their success in that goal more certain. They follow the prescribed route of taking on smaller goals along the way - maybe including in their training a spot of cross training, or other land-based strength work, possibly taking on other unrelated goals along the way to help mix things up a bit. Every goal brings them closer to their ultimate objective. These prescribed routes are well documented and often plans can be adopted verbatim from previous successes in the goal in question. Currently, I know of many people who are following this route, and I think it is a great way to tackle – for some – what is essentially the pinnacle of their careers or goals. Some may only have this goal in mind and the previous years are all moving them along the direction of achieving this single goal.

Whilst the above route is well subscribed to by a vast amount of people, it does come with inherent dangers, which I have seen first-hand, most commonly, burnout and injury. Whilst it is the much easier route to get to a goal, for others, who suffer from lack of focus, other methods have to be adopted.

Some people suffer from impatience and struggle with long term goals, and prefer to not just edge out of their comfort zone but build their own trebuchet in their comfort zone, jump on board, and catapult themselves into another dimension. For these people (I class myself as one of them) decisions are made on impulse and whilst there may be considerable thought going into it, decisions are made very quickly, often with little regard to what you have actually done.

A chat with my brother was long overdue, not something he and I do unless there is something really bothering us, so we met up, and sat down. I brought up this Channel swimming madness. Since our initial talk about it, he had moved on and was beginning a family but was still whole heartedly behind the idea of me doing it. It turns out I can be a real sucker for punishment.

When you look at something like a big goal in life, the pros and cons may not be apparent at the time, and for the impulsive person, this list will only cover a very short time period and the goals will be on an equally ludicrous timescale. After all the swimming I had been doing and given the base I had measured, this goal looked like a very viable option to fix my quandary, "How to get fit quickly?" Swimming the English Channel now started to look like a pretty enticing concept.

For the impulsive amongst us, there may be other reasons why we take on these goals over such short time frames. It could be the fact that a "normal" challenge is just not big enough to get you to focus properly. You have to really push the boat out to get that focus. If you are blessed with a natural athletic ability but also suffer from being extremely lazy, it sometimes requires something which looks totally insurmountable to get you off the sofa. For my part, the fear – which was very real - was lacking the stamina to follow through by losing focus along the way or possibly suffering burnout.

The following weeks were spent tracking down articles of people who had taken on this challenge. I devoured blogs and write ups of Channel crossings and the challenge I was setting myself now started to come into focus. What started out as a bit of a fact-finding mission, now became an obsession. An obsession that provided a lot more questions than answers! I was doing my Masters training three times a week, but the mileage I was putting in was falling very far short of others that were attempting to take on the same challenge. My inexperience in this field became acutely apparent. Nearly all who were attempting this goal had a good few swims under their belt, many of them had already taken part in relay swims, and the majority were already accomplished open water swimmers. Some had dedicated coaches and others mixed their training up with other land-based activities. My despondency grew. With a job and a life to lead, I was very far from where all the literature prescribed I should be. Maybe I had bitten off more than I could chew? Maybe this is a sport for extraordinary people? Maybe I was just a charlatan trying to be something I am clearly not? But with the growing despondency, my obstinate streak was also growing. Then in October 2007, I decided. If you never try you will never know, so stop prattling around with all this "should we shouldn't we" stuff and make a decision one way or the other.

It was now time to throw all caution to the wind and pick up a phone and start enquiring about boat hire. I was aware that there were two bodies that you could sign up with to do the English Channel. One was the CSA (Channel Swimming association) which had been around for decades and was the go-to organisation to do this type of event. There was also a newly formed organisation called the CS&PF (Channel swimming and Piloting federation). I was not too concerned about which one to join, but because an aspiring Channel swimmer I had met had signed up with the CS&PF, this is the organisation that I went with. I had found out too that they ran a training camp throughout the summer in Dover harbour, a dedicated group of people, which, at the time, was headed up by the great Freda Streeter. She was considered the oracle of Channel swimming, affectionately known by all that know her as the Channel General. Freda is also the mother of the Queen of the channel, Alison Streeter, who holds the record for the most Channel crossings by a female. Her son has his own boat that he uses to pilot swimmers across to France. Freda and her merry bunch of helpers were at the beach every Saturday and Sunday and Bank Holiday, come rain or shine, throughout the summer, starting in early May to help Channel swimmers towards their goal.

As it was so late in the year, (and this is now often the case), all tides were booked - getting a pilot to take me across the English Channel was proving harder than I expected. However, there were a few pilots who were waiting on confirmation and they said they would get back to me. The costs high but with some serious saving, we would just be able to afford it. At prices ranging between £2600 and £3500 - *just to hire a boat* – I started thinking that sailing and horse riding might actually be the cheaper of the sports that I had done. This challenge was well beyond me both physically and mentally and now, I was beginning to realise that the financial costs were high. I am not trying to put anyone off. When you break that cost down, it is very reasonable, really. For that price, you get a boat, its crew, its diesel and an observer. If you break that price down into an hourly cost, as some people will have the boat for twenty four hours or more, that's less than £100 per hour. That is pretty good value for money. Looking at it as a lump sum makes it look expensive. At this point I decided to put together a Pros Vs Cons list, now that I had prices and details of what was required. The results were pretty dismal! If I did live my life by spreadsheets alone, the answer was blatantly obvious. This was a REALLY stupid idea. The idea was shelved – for a while. Then, in November of 2007 I got a phone call from one of the pilots, none other than Alison Streeter, the Queen of the Channel. I was reminded of the records under her swimsuit straps which include:

Most crossings – 43
First woman to swim the channel 3 ways
Most crossings in a season – 7
International Swimming hall of fame inductee

She had hung up her swimming trunks and was now entering into the Channel piloting game. My gain! When it came to having an experienced person on the boat, they did not come more qualified than Alison! My channel adventures were getting off to a pretty good start.

She informed me that she had a slot available at the end of the swim season – the Channel swimming season usually kicks off at the end of June, early July, and runs through to late September, early October, weather depending. One of her swimmers had pulled out. I was told that the slot was on a spring tide and usually, swimmers were not booked on these tides but rather on neap tides. The difference between a neap tide and a spring tide is to do with the moon's position in relation to the earth and the resulting gravitational pull. In layman's terms, during a spring tide, the difference between low and high tide is at its greatest, and on a neap tide, the difference is at its lowest. If you look at the English Channel, the distance between Dover and Cap Gris-Nez is twenty-one miles. The tide turns about every six hours. On a spring tide, there is an extra 1.5m of water that squeezes through the English Channel every six hours before it turns 180 degrees and then is squeezed back through the same gap. All that extra water moving in a similar time increases the speed at which the tide is flowing. As the flow of water is fast, it is very common for a tide to turn and, if you are not a fast enough swimmer to make headway across that running tide, you are left with the only option of swimming parallel to the French Coast until the time eventually turns again and dumps you on French soil.

Historically, the spring tides were rarely used, but with the growing popularity of the sport and the short window of the season, they were now being used more frequently and definitely favoured the faster swimmer.

Although I was aware of these things, I took no notice of them. The tides, while important, were not the only thing that would have a great bearing on failure or success. Pilots usually book four swimmers in a seven day period and you are allocated a slot from one to four. Slot one is the first to go and then, weather and elements permitting, the rest follow in quick succession. If you bear in mind that some weeks in the middle of the season can be totally blown out due to poor weather, there will be times when the pilots will literally escort a swimmer over to France, transport them back to Dover and immediately pick up another swimmer to escort them across, spending days at sea. Their job is to monitor the weather and make a call as to whether it will be worth going across or not. The ultimate decision of to swim or not mostly lies with the swimmer themselves whom are merely advised by the pilots on how the conditions are looking. Swims average about fifteen hours and a lot can happen in that time, so what might look like a perfect day can very quickly turn into a gale force winds. By monitoring the weather patterns as far out as the Atlantic, pilots try to assess and gauge what the patterns will do, and then make a call as to the possibility of making a crossing. This is the reason why you can be sitting around for a few weeks without a viable weather window to give you the opportunity to safely get across to France - even though conditions in Dover might very well be idyllic, out in the Channel, it could be blowing a gale. This is the one serious downside of Channel swims, especially if you have flown halfway across the globe to attempt the swim. Not only does it cost a small fortune sitting around waiting, but it can play havoc with the months, sometimes years of training that you have put in. This is where the mental game starts, as the waiting can really create chaos with your mental fortitude.

The slot that Alison offered me just happened to fit perfectly with a trip that my parents were making over to the United Kingdom. I could make this a family affair! My parents had pretty much given up their lives to follow my brother Spencer and I around the globe on our sporting endeavours, so it was time to treat them for once. What more could anyone want than to be sitting on a boat going 2.5 miles per hour across one of the busiest shipping lanes in the world? All whilst getting buffeted by the elements in the form of rain, wind and waves? I am such a nice son!

Now it was crunch time for me. Was I ACTUALLY going to do this? Everything in my life was telling me **not** to do it but there was something in my head that said YES, GO FOR IT. Before I knew it, I was agreeing to swim across to France. The next few nights were sleepless, thinking "Oh My Lord!!! What have I just done?"

Next stop was to fill out all the forms and the registration fee (another cost I had overlooked), and get a medical done (more money!), and probably start training. I now had ten months to go from zero to Channel swim fit. Bearing in mind I hated the taste of saltwater, and I really did not like swimming in cold water, WHAT THE HELL WAS I THINKING?!! The biggest issue I had at that point in time was that my head was totally in the wrong place. This had all happened so quickly that I had not had a lot of time to reflect on whether I was actually *thinking*.

Again, for many, the usual route is to take a few years to take on this challenge. But one thing I want to stress is that there is no book on how to swim in Endurance events. Unlike other sporting endeavours, where there are plenty of books and guides written on how to get from zero to 5km or 10 km, in marathon swimming it is mostly personal accounts of how others have done it - written by some with professional expertise, and others who have managed to do it but lack all forms of scientific or professional qualifications in this field. The reasoning behind this thought process is that there are many ways to approach challenges – be they big or small. Some like to take the time and build up to an event in their lives and take on smaller events along the way, and this is a great way to do it. It develops your ability to focus, not rush, and more importantly improves your self-confidence. With every event this will grow, and your belief in yourself will also grow. Others basically jump in at the deep end and either sink or swim – excuse the pun. A bit like how I was taught to swim. Being the youngest of our group of neighbours, I was always picked on and thrown in the deep end. The choices were clear, learn to swim or drown! It is a very risky approach to take, but with the fear of my lack of focus hanging over me, it was the only way I knew how to approach things. This challenge and my chosen approach began to intrigue me. In the past I had been known to make decisions on impulse and often had my mother freaking out as to how the heck I was ever going to achieve or carry out said decisions. This was different - I had only ever cast myself this far out of my comfort zone once before. That was when I left Africa to go and travel the world, my chosen destination being Antibes in France. I arrived with a backpack, a couple of hundred pounds in my wallet and the belief that I was invincible. I knew nothing about Europe and had no contacts there, so after booking into a hostel, I now had to find a job and start a new life from nothing. This completely freaked my mother out. She wanted me to try and get a job and accommodation organised before I left Africa, but my attitude was, I will just arrive, take one day at a time, and things would turn out fine. Her concerns were as follows:

Mother: 'Where will you stay?'

Me: 'I don't know, probably on a beach if I have to.'
Mom: 'How will you find a job?'
Me: 'I don't know, probably ask around in the harbours.'
Mom: 'What if you can't find a job?'
Me: 'I will find something.'

But that experience had been twelve years earlier. Since then I had had various knocks from life, but while it was nothing I could not cope with, this journey was going to be on a similar sort of level.

One thing that I have learnt along this journey is what works for me may not work for you. Each of us is individual and takes on challenges in different ways for different reasons, and the way we approach it is highly dependent on our individual circumstances.

Inspiration can come from many areas in our lives. We may have seen someone do something and thought WOW; I wish I could do that. Peer pressure might be a factor in some cases. Proving a point to oneself is often another factor that compels people into doing the impossible or proving a point to someone else. It may be a long, deep seated desire to do something. It could be to do with a charity drive, an illness, a route to better health, a challenge to those with poor health. It does not matter how you get the inspiration or where you get it as long as you do. Some people do it for the wrong reasons as well, and some do it just because they can. I think I fit into the latter. It is there, I need to get fit, and this is a challenge that will at least keep me focused and training. We all do things for our own reasons.

So with a new goal set, I now needed to figure out pretty much everything about how to swim to France. The goal that I had set for myself seemed insane to many (I am one of those), but goals should be set on one's own ability. For someone like me with a lazy disposition, the likes of small 3km and 5km swims, or running a marathon, did not have the desired effect of scaring me into keeping focused. The key here was to believe in one's capabilities. The challenge of swimming one of the biggest swims in the world in a timeframe of ten months seemed daunting and verging on madness, but I knew deep down that I needed to do this if I wanted to keep the focus up, otherwise I would do what I had always done - drift through on a wing and a prayer and rely on what little fitness I had to get me through.

With the challenge set, my mind now turned to the next tasks – which were numerous and very scary.

The list of things I needed was immense and included the following:

1 – Where do you start?

2 – Do I need a coach or not?

3 – How am I going to afford this?

4 – Do I need to do land based and water-based training?

5 – How am I going to fit this all into an already busy life?

6 – What is everyone going to think about this?

7 – Who are the best people to approach?

8 – How can I maximise my chances to succeed?

9 – What – if anything, am I going to gain from this?

10 – How can I make this worthwhile for all involved?

The least scary was the training. The bigger question was how on earth am I going to get into the right headspace, to believe I was worthy of doing this challenge and also that I deserved to enter such an elite group? Saving had now become a huge priority to carry me through all of this and how was I going to maintain the momentum needed to do this? It was clear that the following year was going to be very different to previous years. The sacrifices that I would have to make seemed huge – on paper. Time with my friends would have to be curtailed. Time with my family would be limited due to training. Although daunting, the main thing is the journey had begun, and now it was just a matter of enjoying it. Yes, I do my sports for enjoyment!

Let's start with the first question.

1. So where do you start?

Swimming three times a week was already part of my life and had been for the last couple of months. I had already started the journey. Swimming with a Masters class however was going to fall well short of the mark when it came to training. My inspiration came from the fact that I needed to get fit quickly. For me this needed a pretty big goal - I already knew smaller ones did not really get me to focus properly.

I had done the risk analysis, the pros and cons list, and knew that for many reasons this was beyond me - but I still had nine months and a deep drive that said I needed this in my life for the sole purpose of improving my overall health. I had a pilot to get me across, it was now just a process of enjoying the journey that was about to unfold for me. I really had no idea of what the journey ahead held. Sometimes that in itself can be a massive driving force - just to see what is around the next corner or over the next hump. The next thing was to inform people that I was **SWIMMING TO FRANCE.** Pay attention to the exact wording! For most I told, it was met with scepticism. This was unsurprising to me, as I had always been a big talker and although my friends are all very amazing people, the way I lived my life and the way I talked, did not really make me a prime candidate to do this. In all honesty, I think none of them really believed that I was going to do it. There were a few who were supportive at first and remained so throughout, but mostly there was a lot of doubt involved. How my friends thought was immaterial, as long as

I could muster the belief in myself - that is what really mattered.

Once you start talking about a goal, it becomes more real in your mind and the more you talk about it the more real it becomes. Another way to make it real is to write it down, sometimes a few times a week. Again, the wording makes a huge difference. I know of some people who write their goals on their headboard of their beds, on the mirror in the bathroom. Sounds daft? There is a very subtle yet hugely influential reason for this. It is the very first thing they see in the morning and the very last thing they see before they go to sleep.

2. **Do I need a coach or not?**

This was a serious consideration for me, as I felt that I had a lot to do in a short space of time. The gym where I trained had some good coaches and some of them offered their expertise to coach me, but if I was going to have a coach, they only really needed to meet one criterion: they had to have taken part in some form of ultramarathon distance event taking longer than fifteen hours of exertion.

As I had just entered into this world of open water swimming, I did not know many Ironman triathletes or open water swimmers, so there was really no one at the gym who could coach me. So, I decided that I would not employ the services of one. This would also save money to put towards this challenge. I needed to throw everything at this. Having trained fairly competitively during another era of my life and having been a competitive swimmer many moons ago, I had some idea of how to train – definitely not for something like this, but I had a rudimentary idea of how to do it and was looking forward to refining not only my swimming skills, but also taking the knowledge that I had and expanding on it. Again, another aspect of the journey that became pretty enjoyable.

Now, looking back on my past, I do think coaches are a great benefit and offer you a hell of a lot more than sets. In the world of sports today, to get anywhere in your sport, there are now massive benefits from other aspects rather than just doing the miles. Diets, cross training, hydration, and many other things need to be addressed to be able to get through a big event. Although I have never hired a coach per se, the benefits can be significant, and I learnt this on my most recent ultra- distance swim, Loch Lomond. I already had my support crew lined up, but Robert Hamilton of Vigour Events in Scotland, an open water swim coach, joined my team at the very last minute. He did not know my ability, but the tough love that was dished out at about midnight when I began to develop hypothermia, was probably the key to taking a swim that in my mind was a certain failure to a successful 11.5 hours in 13-14°C (or 55-57° Fahrenheit) water. If he had not been there, my team would not have known how to handle the effects of hypothermia - and being my immediate family (wife and brother), I think they would have urged me out of the water rather than have to deal me some serious tough love. Robert is now known as the only Glaswegian that I have threatened to punch multiple times if he got himself close enough to the water for me to deliver it!

Each athlete is totally different in their approach, but I think there are three questions that need to be asked:

1 – Figure out where you are at. I had already done this, I knew I was overweight, unfit and required a LOT of work. I also knew that I could float around a pool pretty well. I had done some benchmark tests on my ability, so knew where I was on that front.

2 – Define where you want to be. In this instance, it was clearly to be standing on the shores of France.

3 – Decide how you are going to get there.

For the above three points, the first one can easily be done without a coach. In the pool on your own, you can time yourself over various distances at a comfortable pace to see what sort of times you are getting, or look in the mirror.

Point two is where a coach can be very useful to sit down with and figure out a game plan and a time frame, and then an overall plan can be developed. A coach is by no means essential, but for many, it is a necessary sounding board to agree where you are in your journey. At this time, I considered my very shaky knowledge on building a training plan and altering my stroke - by comparing my stroke to those of the greats, it was immediately obvious that there was a lot of work that needed to be done, but the basics were definitely there. My times that I had gathered as my base were by no means terrible, so were a decent point from where to start.

The third point is now where I was at and I figured that as I would be swimming to France, the best form of training was, swim, swim some more and then swim again. I was running out of time, and fast. I had been reading blogs voraciously and others that were doing the same challenge as I was were already SO FAR ahead of me in pretty much everything with regards to this challenge. I was not going to "waste time" on other forms of training as I was not going to run to France, or cycle to France, or paddle to France. SWIM is what I needed to do, so that is pretty much all I did.

This is where a coach can really make a difference, by defining sets for you, implementing targets and goals and also – if you are lucky enough to have your coach poolside when you swim - driving you through and keeping you focused and motivated. It can be far easier to have someone take on this responsibility and leave you as the athlete to do the work. They can also be good at issuing out a bit of tough love when it is needed. Doing it within a group it makes the tedium more bearable and you will find yourself flying through your training plan. Coaches will usually have the training to help you tweak your stroke to keep you improving. They can offer tips and drills to help you overcome and change your bad habits and move you from thrashing through the water to gliding through it.

Many now offer video analyses, and this can be a no brainer when it comes to improving stroke technique. Often, all that is required is for them to film you in the water from different angles, then sit down with you and get *you* to critique your own stroke. I have done this before with swimmers and you will be amazed at how good they are at critiquing their own stroke, especially when you offer the ability to watch themselves, followed by a much more accomplished swimmer. While people are generally very good at picking out their flaws, they may not have the wherewithal to make the changes, and this is where a coach will come in.

When it comes to ultra-distance swimming, technique can mean the difference between a 10 -12 hour swim and a 16 – 18 hour swim. If money is your concern, I would spend it on technique training rather than an expensive personal trainer, who might not be a swim coach and just issue you with a heavy load of long sessions in the pool. Not only will a better technique improve your overall time, but it will also reduce the amount of energy used to cover that distance. Another benefit from an efficient stroke is the lower risk of injury to your body. If you watch some of the great swimmers out there, pool and open water, they make it look so effortless.

Although there are some exceptional coaches out there who can work on your technique with great success, they may have no idea about the mental requirements to get you through a 10 – 20 hour challenge. As human knowledge grows, however, professionals often develop their area of expertise and focus on that entirely so taking advice from different coaches can be necessary to focus on different areas of your challenge.

By *not* having a coach, you can still have access to a wealth of information on sets, drills, technique tips and information on how you can improve your stroke. There are loads of videos on how to swim faster, better, and on many other areas that can be improved. This relies on you being able to critique your own stroke, and then understand how the drills and tweaks need to be carried out.

My technique, which I thought was not that great, seemed reasonably efficient fortunately in comparison to the others that I used to train with, and I was on average about 15min per 1000m, so about 4000m per hour. I was comparing myself to two other groups - the masters I swam with but also the plethora of blogs and sets that I was reading on the internet. Not the greatest idea, but it was all I had at my disposal. This is where I learnt that the internet is a bit of a double-edged sword!

There are vast quantities of blogs now out there with regards to endurance events. The ones I read were about people who had been doing this long-distance swimming for years – I had never done anything like this! Other blogs were written by competitive swimmers and clearly they were all way ahead of me. Just reading about all those experiences made me feel really low, as I was in a totally different league; out-swum, outclassed and nowhere near where I was meant to be – according to these oracles. I didn't realise at the time that with many of these big challenges, most people choose the only option they know - train more, swim longer, swim harder, do more physical preparation.

It eventually dawned on me that to follow posts on social media was not helpful. In the words of Baz Luhrman song, 'Always wear sunscreen', "don't read beauty magazines, they will only make you feel ugly!" Allow me to elaborate. In the past, I followed social media posts religiously but all they did was make me feel terrible about myself. When I read what others who were doing the same challenge were getting up to, it only left me feeling wanting and completely despondent as I was well off the mark. Rookie error! I stopped reading these posts and instead went to train with a few others who were training for similar events and I soon realised that yes, they might be doing the big distances but their intensity was pretty poor. My training so far had been high intensity, low mileage. All I was doing was taking another approach - it was by no means wrong, just different.

We are all the same with regards to outside influence and it was at this point where I made a pact with myself. Based on my religious teachings, one writing from the bible came back to my mind, and it was St Paul's letter to the Romans, chapter 12, verse 2, which reads as follows. *"Do not model yourselves on the behaviour of the world around you, but let your behaviour change, modelled by your new mind."*

I was going to do this my way and do it to the best of my ability. I was not going to be influenced by anyone out there that I did not know or trust. Not that I did not admire all these swimmers who were doing anywhere between 30km and 50km of swimming a week. I was not in that league for many reasons and I did not know their circumstances. I had realised that to compare yourself to anyone is pointless and will only result in one outcome - self-esteem will drop, doubts will start to creep in and depression sets in - and once you let it get a grip, it can take years to shake off.

STOP READING BLOGS. Any challenge of this magnitude is huge for anyone so trying to compare yourself to others is a fast track to being unsuccessful. I am not saying you must ignore any advice, but be ruthless about which advice you choose to take on board.

It seems now that with the advent of the internet, we are constantly marvelling at other people's choices and successes. There is no shortage of "Photoshopped" lives out there. Lives that seem full of success, joy, jubilation and triumph. It is human nature to put your best foot forward and be admired - we are all guilty of it. The reality is usually very different from what is broadcast. What is not regularly broadcast to the world – or even very close friends – are the trials and tribulations, hard work, blood, sweat and tears that has to happen for the fifteen minutes of fame, be it on general or social media. By all means, if you are going to read social media posts, take them with a pinch of salt.

I digress. So - do you need a coach? Well, if you feel that it will be useful to have someone guiding you, then go ahead and get one. For others (this includes me), I am very happy to train on my own and I am also confident enough to build my own training sets. During my training, twice a week I would join in my Masters group for a bit of variation. I would arrive about an hour and a half early and then hammer out a pretty brutal set on my own with no one else around, and then use the Masters group as a bit of a fun session or warm down. By the time they started I had generally done anywhere between 4 and 6km. I was only doing about 15 – 20km a week split between about 3 -4 sessions that did not last longer than about 2 hours at a time.

Another vital aspect of swimming is to keep on testing your technique. People who take on marathons – of any kind – fit into very different spectrums. You have those that learnt from a very young age and have been doing it all their lives, so in general, their technique is very good and they are able to play with that technique whilst they are in a training set, or in an event. On the opposite end of the scale, you have those that have come into the sport very late and they might be able to do the sport in question, but their technique lets them down. I remember arriving at a training event one year and I met a person who was the epitome of a swimmer - tall, broad shoulders long extension - but they were really slow in the water. Then there were others who looked like they really needed to get into some form of exercise but were amazing swimmers, who could do 50m in 30 seconds. So, technique is a vital part of success in any event and if you have the wherewithal to get professional technique training, then do it.

With good technique, you then have the ability to tweak it during the event to match the conditions that you are experiencing. In any 10 – 20 hour swim, you are always at the mercy of the elements - especially with a swim like the Channel, where the weather and conditions can change in a few hours. You could start in very calm waters and within hours you could be swimming in force five or six wind. The stroke that you use to get through the flat water and the stroke used to get through 6 – 10 feet waves that are crashing onto you from either side is very different. Another time to adapt your stroke is when pain niggles set in or an old injury starts to play up. The ability to switch your stroke to the conditions is crucial. It is a handy tool to have in your arsenal when you hit the proverbial wall. I am lucky, or maybe unlucky enough to have been in a situation where I did hit that wall, and the ability to get me through that was not only my amazing crew but also being able to switch my technique and mental attitude when I needed to.

When it comes to selecting a coach, as you can see, I am not really up to speed with that as I chose not to go with one. I figured that if someone was going to coach me, they would at least have to have done a swim in excess of 25km in the ocean. In those days, there were not a lot of those around (that I knew of) so I decided to go it alone. I also figured that an ultra-distance event is more of a mental challenge, and your average coach can very easily help on the physical front but once you enter the ultra-distance, unless they have experienced it, they generally may not have a lot further to offer. I was lucky enough to have already trained in the art of maximising my mental capacity to get me through such things. The techniques which I learnt I use on a daily basis to get me through life's challenges, not just swimming ones.

Nowadays, in all sports, the importance of a more holistic approach to training is becoming more and more apparent, with a huge push towards what they refer to as mindful training. This is a great thing. It's really not about just doing all the physical stuff but spending a lot more time on the psychology of the training. This is one thing that I feel that has always been overlooked in the past.

Having been in this sport for ten years, I have met and swum with loads of people and the one thing that really intrigues me is the fact that you can have some amazing swimmers who are at the pinnacle of their physical fitness, have clocked up hundreds, in some case thousands of hours in pools, lakes, oceans - but they really struggle to get through a 10 – 15 hour swim. It is definitely NOT their physical ineptitude, so it has to be more of a mental block that exists.

3. How am I going to afford this?

With endurance events, this is definitely the elephant in the room. I may wax lyrical about the benefits of doing something like this and how this whole journey has been a phenomenal experience, but it all comes at a cost. I gave up sailing and horse riding due to the expense and I looked for a sport that would require little funds. I needed a sport that would keep me challenged so I went into swimming. However, because the small events held no challenge big or scary enough to force me to train effectively, I fell into ultra-distance events. I probably should have stuck to horse riding and sailing!

Looking at the money I had available, this was a very stupid idea. I could not afford this - I could barely afford to keep my gym membership going, let alone ALL the other expenses that would be heading my way. This is where you have to believe in yourself. I was amazed at how many people rallied around to help me, specifically my family and particularly my wife Rachelle who at the time not only supported this mad idea of mine but gave up a lot to get me through it. Soon I was able to get the money together on the basis that I would run a charity drive, and that all funds raised would be given to the charity. Somehow, I managed to get the financial support that I needed to be able to do this and at the end, still give the charity all the money that I raised. One company that has helped me consistently throughout the years is Okapi Technology. It is owned by a school friend of mine, Colin Durrant, who has been an entrepreneur for the last 20 years. He is also an avid triathlete, taking part in many Ironman distance events. For most the time I have been in this sport, he has helped me out with some funds. All it takes is for one person to believe in you and you can go a long way.

Where there is a will, there is a way, and all you have to do is to go and look for the people and organisations that will be able to help you - and yes, it may take a lot of looking and a lot of negative responses, but in the end, if you get people on board, and make them a part of the event and the journey, it can be done. Just be prepared for the negative responses as there will be many, especially if this is your first dalliance into these events.

These events remain fairly niche and this is one of the reasons that it is not available to the mass market. The costs are significant and there will be a lot of sacrifices along the way. In my opinion, these sacrifices are worth it in the long term.

4. Do I need to do land-based as well as water-based training?

One way of going about any of these events is to just do what you need to do, and in this case, it was swim.
Retrospectively, I can see the benefits of land-based training, and nowadays I do mix things up with Pilates. This is not for the reason of improving my fitness, although it is really helpful to work on the core muscles that are essential to maintaining your stroke; it was more importantly to give me a timeout from life and concentrate more on my breathing and relaxation, both extremely important in swimming and endurance.

Many others will mix in gym and strength training. I do not do any gym work unless I end up in a situation where I need to. Everyone who has – or is going on a journey to do something like this - is INDIVIDUAL. Your circumstances are not mine. Your life pressures are not mine. Your time constraints are not like mine. Each of us is unique and our lives are all different, as are our abilities. Do what suits you, but consider both land-based training and water-based training as they can go a long way to making training less monotonous. This is crucial when you have a long-term goal - mix things up and KEEP IT INTERESTING. What can break up the tedium of swimming long sets is to throw in some land-based training *during* your swim training. If the pool will allow it, after each set, get out and do twenty press-ups, after the next set, twenty sit-ups, and burpees, run around the pool – if you have access to a pool that is not restrained by health and safety protocols.

In my circumstances, with nine months to get swim fit, there was only one option for me: JUST KEEP SWIMMING, JUST KEEP SWIMMING, JUST KEEP SWIMMING. So there was no land -based training involved when I was training for the Channel. During the winter it was all done in the pool and when the summer arrived, I moved into the lakes and the ocean.

5. How am I going to fit this all into an already busy life?

Well, if you want to take on any huge challenge in life and still continue your life as you know it, NEWSFLASH – you are setting yourself up for failure! Anything you do will involve sacrifice. It will take time and it will take effort. So of all the balls you are juggling at the moment, you might as well put some aside. For any challenge in life, if you want it to be a fulfilling, it will require a life change.

This is one of the reasons I do not diet as I believe they will not work. Yes, you can change your eating regime and your training regime, get to your required weight and then resume your old life. I personally do not know anyone who has successfully dieted and then resumed their old life and kept the weight off. If you want something to be life changing, you need to change your life - and for the effects to be long term, the changes need to become an integral part of your life going forward. You might be experiencing a midlife crisis and this will be your only challenge, but the effect will be life changing. I do not know many that have a goal of this magnitude and then never do a single thing after it. Take on something like this and you will be a changed person.

If you are going to start changing your life, you might as well make it fun and engaging. There are two common afflictions that I see with these sorts of goals. Nowadays, these goals are usually have a very long time frame. With open water swimming becoming more and more mainstream, swims fill up fast, not only Channel swims, but many of the more iconic short swims now sell out in a matter of hours. If you were to try and book a boat to cross the English Channel now, the earliest slot you would get is 2021. There is the option of waiting for a slot to be given up, but you then have to be very flexible with your time and for many, keeping up training when you have no idea when you might get to swim is mentally excruciating. It is common now for something like this to be termed a three-year goal! Personally, knowing myself, I could never do it, as I like to have fairly short-term goals. If you are going to dedicate 3 years of your life to something, you better learn, or get help, to make it interesting, engaging and FUN. I see so many people who take on a goal like this then read blogs and take on a mammoth training schedule, only to have it all come crashing down due to losing interest or injury. It is one of my biggest bugbears. Someone will make the decision and book a pilot boat for 2021, get all hyped up in the early stages and take on some mammoth swims as their energy levels and enthusiasm are high. As time goes by, there are commonly two things that happen. Firstly, their enthusiasm wanes, the training becomes erratic and with the distance done, complacency sets in. The second affliction is injury, and if this happens early on in your journey, it could end your journey altogether.

6. What is everyone going to think about this?

At the end of it all, who cares? As long as the challenges you set yourself are going to help you grow as a person and make you a better person moving forward, other people's thoughts should not matter. For many of you, your close friends and colleagues may not know anyone who has taken on such a life changing decision and the thoughts of others will range from you being totally mad and having lost all sense of reality, to others being in awe that someone they know will be taking on something like this. If you are going to let other people's opinions matter, then make sure it is the people close to you. Taking on something that is going to affect you so much will ultimately affect your family as well. There will be times in any challenge where emotions will run high and making sure your immediate family are on the same page as you are is imperative. There will also be time spent apart and in the frenetic world we already live in, time is the most precious commodity we have. This is your challenge - no one else's opinions are valid for your goals. If you are going to take notice of opinions, make sure you are taking note of opinions from people who mean something to you and whose lives will be affected.

For any challenge in life, there will be those that are behind you and there will be those that think it is ludicrous. The idea is to follow your own heart and ignore the naysayers. The next thing is to surround yourself with those that are going to make you feel great about your challenge and embrace it with you. These are the people that are ultimately going to get you through it. You do not want people that are going to put doubts into your head and you do not want people who are going to put you down. Most of all, avoid people that are negative about your challenges. There is a fine line between negativity and constructive criticism, the latter being very useful to cement the challenge in your mind.

Having trashed social media, this is where it can be very useful, as you can sign up to the plethora of groups out there made up of people that are on the same journey as you. These are excellent places to ask questions, share ideas and most importantly, put your fears out there and then be ruthless with the responses that you get to those questions.

One thing that struck me the other day when I was looking at a feed on social media on one of the many swimming groups out there; someone had a query about open water and their fears. There were literally hundreds of comments and among them was a comment that made me think. It went as follows: "Such a supportive group, with hundreds of comments - and there is no foul language or abuse!" I think you will agree that social media can be a nasty place to hang around. There are a lot of bitter people out there who seem to have nothing better to do than to post obtuse comments about things. For the most case, sporting groups are generally very supportive and will engage in good and positive discussion.

It is also another great place to forge long lasting friendships. In any challenge out there, we live in a world where whatever you are taking on has most likely been done, so there will be others who have been in your exact position in the past and can give guidance as to how to approach the way you are feeling. Depending on your age, you might very well have been told not to talk to strangers. In today's modern world, you can be having a very engaging conversation with someone on the other side of the world whom you may never meet. Just be aware that not everything on the internet is for real.

7. Who are the best people to approach?

A journey like this will bring you into contact with all sorts of people, both from the world of the challenges and also a few other places along the way.

For the best advice, speak to the people who are in the know. Take time to get to know "who is who in the zoo", figure out their credentials and how they are able to help you. For instance, at the gyms, whilst being a great place to meet people who are working hard to keep their fitness up, it is probably not the best place to find people who have taken on challenges like you are planning. However, when you take on some of the bigger swims where groups are involved, it is often the case that you will meet up with some of the greats. One instance of this was when the Slimhippo and I travelled to Arizona to do SCAR (4 lakes in 4 days). The name SCAR is derived from the names of the lakes that you get to swim in

S = Saguaro lake – 9.5 miles

C = Canyon Lake – 9.5 miles

A = Apache lake – 17 miles

R = Roosevelt lake – 6 miles

Strung along the Salt River canyon in Arizona, this is an awesome swim to do and offers a lot of challenges.

The Great Kayak snake. Getting kayaks from the road to the start at Canyon lake

I was very proud that this would be the longest staged swim I have ever done. Not only is this organised by an amazing guy and his merry helpers, but it attracts some very big hitters in the world of open water swimming. This is where I met Elizabeth Fry. Either she did not like motorboats that much or she possibly thought the 42 miles of swimming was not quite enough, so each day she not only did the swim that we were all doing, but decided it would be a good idea to swim back to the start – effectively doubling up on the distance that us mere mortals swam. Over four days she covered 84 miles of swimming! If I thought that was completely nuts, I also met Martin Strel. This man who not only holds the record for the longest river swim, he holds quite a few others! He has swum the Danube (2,860 km or 1,780 miles), the Mississippi River (3,885 km or 2,414 miles), the Argentine - Parana River (3,998 km or 2,484 miles), the Yangtze River (4,003 km or 2,487 miles), the longest river in Asia, and the Amazon River - this was a record-breaking distance of 5,268 km (3,273 miles). This is just a few of his many swims. In true sporting style, for the SCAR challenge, he was not swimming but kayaking for another swimmer. Another very interesting thing about Martin is the reason he got into swimming. He has various books out and his story is very interesting when it comes to finding out why people do what they do.

The Hippos getting ready to take on Roosevelt Lake. Dusk start and swim into the night.

Whilst Masters' classes in swimming might be a great place to sharpen your skills against very accomplished fast swimmers and a great place for you to work on increasing your speed, it may not be the best place to meet and mix with people who are distance swimmers, even though many of them are superb race swimmers. Likewise, in these circumstances, when you show them your mettle, the admiration is totally mutual, with you in awe of their technique and speed ability and them in total awe of the sheer distances that you will be swimming.

On that note, finding the right people can be very dependent on where you are and what is available to you. For many, living where you want to train is not an option, so you get what you can. If your goal is a marathon swim, then it is unlikely that you will get to mix with a similar mind-set at the local lakes as these are normally heavily subscribed to by Triathletes and their training, and yours will be very different.

Look for people in your local area who have done similar things. Endurance sports are a growing area of expertise and there are now not many places on this planet that do not have someone who has done something similar - and yes, most people who have done this are very happy to give advice about how to go about things.

Try to find likeminded people to mix with and they will be a key part of your life moving forward. Whilst searching out these people always be aware that, even though you might find who you believe to be the perfect training partner/mentor, no one's circumstances are entirely similar. In fact it is often the people who have totally different circumstances to yours that can be the most helpful along the way and the friendships that are forged through these interactions are often long lasting.

8. How can I maximise my chances to succeed?

This is very tightly linked to the above. Mixing with likeminded people is a huge advantage, learning how they went about it and what they did. For those lucky enough to live close to an area where they are able to find a group that is moving towards the same goal, take advantage of that, as training with people who have the same goal in mind is a huge morale boost. Seeing people going through exactly what you are going through is massive. Sharing in other people's experiences will only add to your resilience and your focus.

A challenge of this magnitude will challenge you in more ways than you can imagine and going through the emotional highs and lows along the way in the company of likeminded people cannot be underestimated. Sharing in their joys and their low points will only make you stronger. Also with likeminded people around you, you can then learn the reasons why a lot of people do these sorts of events - and that in itself can be a truly inspirational and uplifting experience. As mentioned before, people do these events for many different reasons.

Not only do you have to prepare yourself physically and emotionally, you also need to spend a lot of time on your mental preparation. This is by far the more important part to focus your attention, and the nice thing about this is that it hardly takes any physical effort to be positive. This is a learned skill that very few people are aware of but having it can greatly impact the outcome of your challenges.

If you are fortunate enough to be near a group that is training and being coached for an event like this, show up, shut up and do exactly what you are told. In some of these groups, complaining is not something that will be tolerated. You are there for a reason and often the people helping and guiding you will have a wealth of knowledge in that area. Be enthusiastic. Yes, it can be hard when you arrive and there is a blowing gale and it's pouring with rain and you have to leave the comfort of your car to get in a choppy cold ocean for 6 – 8 hours. Embrace the challenge, keeping the goal in mind and if you are given a six hour training set, do not try to get out after five hours and fifty-five minutes. These guys will show no mercy and will just throw your ass back in for the last five minutes. Spare a thought for the group that remain on shore in the elements to facilitate your being able to do this. Sometimes, in these circumstances, it is nicer to be in the water than out of it. In quite a few of these training groups, they ask for nothing of you but your grit and determination - so give it to them and you will be on a good path to getting there.

If you have the wherewithal to go on one of the many swimming vacations/training camps that have sprung up over the last couple of years, the same rules apply - you are there to get the mileage in, in a controlled environment under the tutelage of some very experienced people. What they offer is vital time to primarily get some distance into your limbs and secondarily surround yourself with people who may or may not be gearing up for their own event, all with their own experiences, and challenges along the way. These camps, whilst being invaluable for many, are not available to all. With the cost of big endurance events, often there is little left over to put yourself in situations where you can surround yourself with people who will inspire you and keep you going. For those that go it alone, it is crucially important to spend time with friends and family who believe in you to keep you going. The last thing you want is for people to doubt you – unless you are of the mind-set that you are out to prove people wrong.

9. What, if anything, am I going to gain from this?

This is possibly the area where most underestimate the outcome. What starts out as a simple goal can turn into a life altering experience. What you get out of doing something like this is entirely in your hands. For some, this may just be a one off challenge which will take over your whole life for a short period of time. You will push yourself further than you ever thought possible and by doing that, it will give you the belief that anything is possible.

For many though, this starts as a simple goal and then develops into a passion and this is how it was for me. I had one goal - to get fit quickly! The secondary goal was to swim to France. I accomplished both, but was then at a huge loss after the event. I went back to my old ways. I did not even feel proud of what I had actually achieved. I was immensely proud of my team and friends and what they had all done for me. Whilst all around me were massively impressed with what had just unfolded, to me it was just another day. I do not want to take away from any big accomplishment that anyone does, but having done some big training swims, this was merely an extension of those big milestones. Not having anything else to look forward to after the event also magnified the downer I had once I had achieved my goal.

It was my friend Simon Grint, who came to my assistance and urged me to take on other endurance events. Simon has been a long-time friend and he followed my efforts along this journey, taking time out of his busy life to pop down to Dover and watch me train. He is not a swimmer, but still he supported me immensely – not the most scintillating experience he has ever had, I am sure, but he took the time all the same. Whilst camping with him and his partner, sitting around a fire and solving the world's problems, we got talking about what next? One thing you need to know about Simon is that when he thinks, he thinks BIG! He also has excellent organisational skills, something I lack in any significant amount. I am happy to do something that involves only me, as then I only have one person to blame - myself! But when it comes to organising things that will involve others, I generally shy away and rather let others take the lead.

The balmy idea that he had made a swim across to France pale into insignificance. It did not involve any swimming but a lot of other endurance related challenges and multiple sports. The very loose plan involved cycling up Britain from Lands End to John O Groats (1074 miles), kayaking across Scotland (60 Miles), running a marathon and five rounds of golf in a day - with the main aim of raising money. Now each of those challenges in their own right is big for most people, but we were aiming to do all these physical challenges in a month – whilst still holding down jobs. Each one held its own challenges and benefits; the cycling and kayaking afforded us the ability to explore the wonderful British countryside in a way many would never get to do.

So thanks to Simon and Mike Bass (another highly organised individual whom I had only met a year or so previously but was amazing in taking on this challenge), the three of us launched 'The Extreme Five', with the unwavering support of our respective partners, who were there for nearly every event to support us. A few others – Sarah Grint – Simon's sister, Graham Williams and Brett Lynch also took part in the individual challenges. Ultimately, my original goal of swimming to France had now developed into a journey that moved onto organising events, and with the leadership of Simon and the hard work of Mike and all our partners and wives, we had a great deal of fun.

Once 'The Extreme Five' was done, I took a break from swimming for a while and took on a few other small challenges that were mediocre compared to what I had just done. None of them pushed my boundaries or held any sense of achievement that I could look on with pride, and I found myself drifting again. Soon I was back to the low times; my marriage to Rachelle broke down and so, in need of some downtime, I found my way back to the water's edge. I would spend many hours often late into the night, sitting and watching the water on the edge of a lake or river or ocean to seek out the safety and solitude that I had achieved when I was doing big swims. Whilst watching water was immensely therapeutic for me, it just did not give me the sense of comfort and safety that I had experienced in the past. It didn't take me long before I realised that I needed to stop looking at the water and get back to BEING in the water. Having the water wrap itself around me was extremely comforting. This was where I was comfortable and this is where I did most of my thinking, dreaming up further challenges for a journey that, to this day, continues unabated. Soon I was back to the bigger challenges, which saw the Slimhippo and I travel to Arizona and Zurich, and now, I am moving onto other areas within the sports world with the aim of inspiring others and helping them to achieve their goals. I have shared my experiences on my blog and website, which hopefully will inspire and give some swimmers assistance and food for thought.

One thing that sport in general has afforded me in my life is the ability to travel to some spectacular places around the world. With so many events now popping up all over the world, I like to travel and experience new places so I do not think there will be a time when I do a challenge I have already done. There are a few exceptions, but I do mostly like to do new challenges, and take on new adventures.

One of the best parts of my journey has been meeting some truly inspirational, fun and truly mad people, which have been such an important part of each of my challenges. The swimming community is an amazing group to be a part of.

10. How can I make this really worthwhile for all involved?

The best way for people to feel useful is for them to be involved. I learnt this from the amazing friends that I have. They have all played a part in getting me to my ultimate goal - some in the form of helping me raise money for my respective charities, some in the form of just joining me for a training swim. Others just made the effort to come and see me after my training swims, but what was the most mind blowing, was when I jumped on Alison's boat to travel to the start of my Channel swim. After doing the necessary paperwork, we arrived at Samphire Hoe – a common starting place for the swim across to France. There on the beach were thirty of my mates (!) who had travelled from different parts of the United Kingdom. Alison then asked who the people on the beach were. I mentioned to her that they were a group of my friends who had come to see me off. I think she was as gobsmacked as I was! She said that in her entire time as an English Channel swimmer, she had never ever seen so many people on a beach to see someone start a Channel swim. One of them - Doug Robinson – (who has always been known to do silly things but is the life and soul of any gathering) was making sure that all there were feeling included.

As the boat pulled up to about 100m from the shore, the plan was for me to jump in and take the short swim to the shore, get out and walk about 5m up the beach and, when ready, signal to the boat. A siren would then sound, denoting the start of my Channel swim. As I waved goodbye to my friends and well-wishers, Doug stripped down to his smalls and decided he was going to swim with me to France. The last thing I heard before my head disappeared into the murky English Channel was, "Gumps, hold on, I am coming with you!" He lasted about 50m before the cold (and his atrocious stroke) forced him to turn back. Sixteen hours later – at 2am on Monday morning, most of these amazing people were still there to welcome me back with champagne and smiles. That whole group played an important part supporting me and made an immense difference to my final preparations - and ultimately to my success.

Every single person on that beach to see me off, whilst they might not realise it, was instrumental in getting me across to the French coast. As part of my charity fundraising efforts, most on that beach had already attended a fundraising garden party that had been organised in my name and had already been extremely generous with their time and their efforts. This made not only my Channel swim a success, but also raised about £6000 for charity. People may not realise it, but by involving them in as many aspects as I could made them feel part of the challenge, and that in turn made them crucial to my success.

As endurance athletes, we are not able to do these challenges on our own - yes we might be a front to the challenge, but we are by no means capable of doing any of it without an army of supporters that take an active or inactive role in the whole journey.

I think the most underestimated and undervalued people in any of these challenges is our support crew – no matter what role they play - and the best way to show your appreciation to all of them is to involve them in as much as you can. We might think that this is all about us as the person doing the event, but we really are nothing without the friends and family that get behind us.

Currently my challenges are a lot more low key and they predominantly involve the Hippo family: Me - the Zimhippo - the person who does the swimming, my wife – the Slimhippo - who is key to all my feeding, planning, support and kayaking, and occasionally my brother, the Pygmy hippo. Together we travel the world taking on little challenges. However, the person who I am most proud of is the Slimhippo. She wanted to be more involved in these events so, to make her part of the team, I asked her to be my support crew on Lake Zurich in Switzerland. We were not sure what support boat she would be getting, but she jumped at the opportunity to come. On the morning of the swim, we ended up with an excellent boat to spend the day on, (just as well, as if she had had to kayak it at that point, our relationship would have been off to a rocky start!) and she loved being part of it. Who wouldn't enjoy drifting down Lake Zurich, sunbathing on the sundeck, sipping a gin and tonic with Wifi at her disposal, occasionally having to muster the energy to throw the Zimhippo a bottle of feed or a treat, if I was able to attract her attention! To her credit, she even jumped in for a short dip with the Zimhippo towards the end. Well, we have got to keep them happy somehow! She honestly thought that this supporting effort was a bit of alright.

It was time to strike while the proverbial iron was hot! A few months later, I asked her if she would be interested in supporting me in a 42-mile staged swim in Arizona - the SCAR swim; four lakes in four days. Knowing how she loves to travel, I knew a chance to visit Arizona would be hard for her to turn down - provided that I tack on a bit of a holiday at the end of it. I then said, "But you would have to kayak the 42 miles, with the longest day being a 17 mile kayak (circa 8 -10 hours)." This is where I thought it would all go wrong and I would be told to pack my bags and go on my own. To my utter amazement, she said yes.

She had never kayaked before in her life and now she had agreed to kayak 42 miles! So another divergent journey had to take place. In amongst my training, I now had to teach the Slimhippo how to kayak and also how to get fit enough to kayak the distance.. In winter. In the United Kingdom! I have never been more amazed at someone's determination to do everything perfectly and I learnt a lot about focus and dedication. It was a far cry from my approach to any little challenge. Most evenings or weekends were spent kayaking up and down the River Wey in the depths of the British winter. I would rather have been in the water than floating on it, but the Slimhippo was determined to get fit for this. After one or two dips in the frigid waters of the River Wey – she was adamant that she wanted to learn how to recover from a capsized kayak. I told her that she was completely bonkers! I was not going to teach her, as I really did not want to go swimming in 3°C water just to teach her how to do it. So, she found a kayaking group who would teach her how to capsize a perfectly good kayak in arctic temperatures and then recover. She did learn and I really admired her tenacity. But no amount of preparation in the arctic waters of the river way in Surrey could prevent the Slimhippo from succumbing to hypothermia - in Arizona of all places!

I learnt a lot about true grit and determination during the above episode and it also made me realise, more than before, that there is always something to learn - even if you do live by the 6 P's regime. What are the 6 P's I hear you ask? *Perfect Planning Prevents Piss Poor Performance*. No matter how much you prepare, there will always be areas that you may have overlooked. This team of the Slimhippo and the Zimhippo was becoming a pretty formidable. With her attention to detail, planning skills and the desire to do everything to the best of her ability, plus my ability to float down a river, lake or ocean, the journey just got a whole lot more fun.

Chapter 6: Training

These next chapters will take into account various aspects of training. Please bear in mind that these are just guidelines as to how it can be done. It is by no means a guaranteed way of how YOU should do it. You are all Individuals, and your training and approach to it should be based on information, gleaned from trusted resources, to build a training regime that will be unique to you. This can involve building your own training sets up as you go, employing the expertise of a professional coach, or researching and getting training sets from the internet. The latter two are the most common approaches. With any endurance training, it can be a lonely sport. Having a coach, or other athletes join you, or just having a set to follow, can be extremely useful. One thing common amongst all long training sets is that they are varied - broken into smaller chunks and involving other strokes or activities to mix it all up a bit. You will be hard pressed to find someone who will just go and swim 10km, without a single break in a pool. The most common way to break that set up is the gruelling 100 x 100m.

It has long been mentioned that any endurance event is 70% mental, 20% physical and 10% luck. So if this is the case, any logical approach to your training would endeavour to use similar ratios within your training, wouldn't it? Sadly, this is definitely not the case, with pretty much everyone favouring the physical side of training and leaving the mental side.

Sadly, if the 70/20/10 is true, then finding information and techniques on training your mind is very hard to find. There are not many people out there who can offer advice on exactly how you can maximise your chances of success by utilising what is probably the most powerful and influential muscle in your entire body - your brain. I think the main reason why mental training is relegated to low priority is multifaceted.

The first and primary reason is that a lot of these courses deal with the mental side of things and there is still a huge stigma attached to anyone who might claim that they are a bit mental. In reality, to do ultra marathons of any description you have to be different to what society deems to be normal. That is the wonderful thing about the human race - there is no such thing as normal, only society's perception on how normal should be. Since time began, society has tried to pigeonhole each and every one of us into a specific way, and those who go against the grain or think differently are often looked at as being rebels. It is often those people that go on to achieve great things. So why would anyone want to be normal? You should constantly strive to be the best you that you can possibly be. Often people on the path of enlightenment will search out a GURU – (Someone, who I consider to be a Guru at what they do, once asked me to spell GURU. Go on, say it out loud and listen to what you are saying).

The next reason that mental training is so low down on many people's radar is that there is very little you can do to monitor, chart or measure it. There are plenty of monitors available to measure physical progress and development. Smart watches are the latest tech employed to track all your movements, and the data collected can include stroke rate, heart rate, pace, distance covered, cadence, steps done, aerobic versus anaerobic exercise – the list is endless. But to what end? How many people actually analyse all the data and have come up with a way to manipulate that data in a coherent way to improve your overall times? Unless you are at the cutting edge of any sport where you have an army of analysts to crunch the data, the data is, for all intents and purposes, mostly not very useful. Physical training is very much results based, but mental training is very elusive. Few would say with unwavering certainty that engaging in any form of mental preparation made all the difference; or any difference at all. However, in general, you are where you are at today because of your mental ramblings and thoughts and before you do anything, you first have to decide to do it. You can't physically go and do anything and then later think about doing it.

Another reason is the time and energy needed to train. Having been on quite a few courses, learning and teaching how to utilise more of our mental capacity takes a huge initial time investment. If the training courses that I attended over the years were spread out into a more leisurely format, then the impact of the courses could be lost and people would then go away unconvinced. But to get the maximum impact of the training, you need to get from point A to point

Z in a very quick timeframe to create an impact on people's perception as to what our mind is REALLY capable of. Also, the courses generally build on each other and doing it in a guided fashion makes a massive difference.

I think the final reason that mental training is very low down on the agenda is the fact that doing it is very subtle. It may not ever require any form of exercise, (in fact the techniques used by most for training their mental state are done in a very relaxed way, often in a state of meditation or relaxation so you might not get physically tired from undertaking the training) but the results can be enormous, and I have yet to find any athlete that does not believe that mental training is very important. So which technique can actually have the biggest impact? The simple way in which athletes talk about themselves and their goals.

Once techniques are learnt and the results can be seen, then it is up to you as a person to go away and start using them. Whilst I do not physically train on a daily basis, I do spend time on my overall mental preparation every single day of my life, sometimes multiple times a day. This is because it can be done absolutely anywhere - I do not need a gym, Pilates instructor, swimming pool, river, lake or ocean. All I need is 5 minutes or more to make a difference to my overall mental wellbeing.

Physical training

So you are at the point where you have signed up to take on possibly the biggest physical challenge of your life. Let's put it into context:

A marathon - average time 3 – 5 hours

Triathlon Standard - average time 2 -4 hours

Ironman - average time 12 – 13 hours

100mile cycle - between 4 – 10 hours (terrain differences)

English Channel swim - average between 13-16 hours

Ultra-distance swimming is possibly one of the longest single effort events out there. There are obviously others that may be longer, but most of those are staged over a couple of days with time available to rest in between. Recently this has been seriously challenged with the first 104 mile swim in a lake, lasting over 67 hours. Those challenges are ones the majority of us can only dream of. Currently the English Channel is still regarded as the pinnacle of open water swimming. It is often referred to as the Mount Everest of open water swimming, which is odd, considering the facts:

Mount Everest – first summited in 1953 by Edmund Hilary and Tenzing Norgay.

Number of times summited - 9159 (as at December 2018)

Youngest to summit - Jordan Romera, age 13 years 10 months

On average, that is 141 per year since the first summit.

English Channel - first swum in 1875 By Matthew Webb

Number of times crossed - 2126

Youngest swimmer - Tom Gregory aged 11 years 11 months in 1988

Oldest swimmer - Otto Thanning, aged 73 years and 4 months in 2014

You can see that since Mount Everest was first summited, there has been a gain of one hundred and forty per year attaining that accolade of reaching the top of the earth. In contrast, since the first English Channel crossing, there have only been fourteen per year. So, while the two are compared, and associated with being the pinnacle of their fraternities, they are very different beasts. They are both considered to be extreme sports and with both there are the inevitable fraternity rocking fatalities.

There is also the added complication of tides, water temperature, wind, and exposure to the elements for extended periods of time. There are also the challenges of swimming at night, jellyfish, lack of sleep, boredom etc. to overcome. Yes, training for something like that entails a lot of time and a lot of commitment. Luckily assistance is available, and generally run by groups of highly accomplished endurance swimmers who are purely lovers of the sport and hold little or no paper qualifications but are more a collection of likeminded people doing what they love. Do not expect any hand holding from these groups, there is a lot of tough love involved here. Generally you are all heading towards a similar goal and the feeling of "we are all in this together" is a powerful element that drives you towards your respective goals.

These groups are an exceptional place to build up your confidence slowly in a controlled environment, where there are always people there who will be available to help you feed, make sure you are doing all right, and from the beginning of the season will build you up slowly from thirty minute dips in the ocean to seven or eight hours in the water. Part of this is due to the fact that for many swims over 20 miles, (32km) there will be an obligatory health and safety requirement to be able to finish at least a six-hour swim in water temperatures below 16°C. Some argue that this minimum requirement should be longer. Another obligation for long distance swims is that you will have to have a medical sign off from a doctor. This is for insurance purposes and the fact that the organising bodies need to know that you are physically able to do this sort of distance.

This last point can be a bit of a minefield as often your General Practitioner (GP) will not sign off on these documents as they essentially may not know your history in these sorts of events and also their insurance might not cover them signing these forms. The costs can range wildly in price if your doctor will indeed sign the papers. It is now becoming mandatory in Europe to have a medical certificate for nearly every open water event, distance being completely irrelevant. I mention this as it can be a big chunk of your budget for these events. At some of the dedicated groups I have mentioned, there are often medically qualified people in the group that will be happy to discuss and possibly sign off on these forms, for a small fee – generally a lot less than your GP would charge you.

Another debate that has been bubbling on is the question - should endurance athletes, by law, have to undergo a full ECG test before being allowed to partake in these events? In my opinion, having talked to a cardiologist friend of mine, the answer is NO. But it remains a controversial point, so this could become part of the requirements in the future.

Now if anything is true, taking part in these dedicated groups is essential if this is your first time doing something like this. It is very easy to underestimate the emotional rollercoaster you will go through when you take on controlled training and reach all the little milestones along the way. While having a lot of physical exposure to time in the water generally builds your confidence, the most useful part is that you slowly build on the time you are in the water. One of the fundamental aims of training is to get you to be doing the effective distance of the channel over two days. So you start at about 40 minutes in the water and over the season, you will go in for up to 6 hours followed by seven hours the following day.

Some people will do eight hours on Saturday then another eight hours on Sunday so over a weekend of swimming will accomplish sixteen hours of swimming in the harbour, lake or ocean.

While these dedicated groups offer you the ability to get your distance up pretty quick, because they are generally run by enthusiasts that have other commitments during the week, they are usually only available at the weekends. It does not mean that you should stop your pool training during the week. Each type of training will offer different aspects to your training regime. Whilst in the pool you may very well focus on shorter distances with the emphasis being on technique, drills and improving aerobic ability. The longer weekend swims will be very useful for the cold water acclimation, dealing with the boredom and swimming in a different environment. The salinity of the ocean is not very pleasant, and offers a very different experience to lake or pool swimming, due to the added buoyancy of the water. So, do not ditch your pool sets just because you are doing much longer sets in the ocean or the lakes.

An important part of pool training is tweaking your technique in a controlled environment and this inevitably brings in the use of swimming aids. This in itself can be contentious, and attracts a lot of discussion. These come in the form of pull buoys, paddles (which range in size from fairly sublime to the utterly ridiculous) kick boards, ankle straps, wrist and ankle weights, centre snorkels, drag pants, parachutes and many others. Personally, I do not use aids apart from a kick board and a pull buoy. However, I do have the best drag pants in the business. A result of a bit of a joke between the Slimhippo and I. After me complaining that I did not have any when I went to a training session, I told her that, if she was any good at her support role she would get me a pair of drag pants. AND SHE DID!!! Believing that I would never ever wear them! OH how wrong she was. The man with the crochet shorts was born.

I must admit, I do not swim in them much as they weigh a ton when wet. My theory toward training aids is that I do not want to gain dependence on them. I do think that aids can be very useful in helping a swimmer adjust their stroke, but my feeling is that they should be used sparingly, and also under the guidance of a coach or tutor.

Over the years there has been a growing industry of swimming holidays that are run in various locations throughout the world by some very experienced open water swimmers. On these you will get to swim in exotic locations and have the luxury of some very good advice. Some are more holiday than swimming, whilst others are more swimming than holiday! Either way, the aim is the same to give you maximum exposure to time in the water and expertise of some very influential people in the game. What you also get is the opportunity to spend time with like-minded people, many of whom are on a similar journey as you. Be aware that these holidays or camps are often carried out in water temperatures that will not prepare you for the bigger colder swims, and while they get you swimming, you will have to do cold water acclimation elsewhere. The opportunity of watching other people going along the same journey can be priceless. You get to see people who are all wrestling with the same emotions and challenges that you are, and you get to learn from them how they deal with their demons. It makes it all the more real and you then realise that it is not just you that has these struggles, but that everyone who takes on these challenges has them, and their ways of dealing with them are very different.

Just swimming with certain people can make the world of difference to your resilience. On a personal note, when I was undergoing the training for the Channel, I was very lucky to share the water with a paraplegic. When we started getting in the longer swims, 3 -7 hours, we used to feed on the hour, every hour. This would entail swimming back to the shore where there was a dedicated group of helpers to feed me some energy drink and treats. This serves two purposes: primarily to get some feed into your system and to also afford the helpers some interaction with you so as to gauge how you are doing.

Now this can be mind numbingly boring and often, after about 3 hours in the water, I used to come back to the shore for a feed by the beach crew. I would be wrestling with my conscience at these points. How can I at least fake that I am not coping very well and hopefully they will ask me to get out and call it a day? I would walk up to the water's edge, get my feed, and then I would see this paraplegic friend arrive for a feed, on her elbows. She would crawl up to the water's edge in the crashing waves (often experiencing numerous scrapes and bruises from the pebbles that are the beach,) take on her food, have a brief interaction with the beach crew, before promptly crawling back into the water for another set. This was a defining moment in my training sessions and a lesson in grit and determination. At this point I had just had enough of this ploughing up and down the course and I just wanted to get out. Then I would see my paraplegic friend. From that moment on, there were two things that shaped my future. I watched this scenario unfold many times over and I told myself, if she can do it, there is no reason unless I am dying, that I cannot do it. I also came up with the question that I asked myself at nearly every feed. It went something like this: If you stop now, are you stopping because you physically cannot go on? Or are you just mentally bored? If it was the latter, then I did not have a good enough reason to stop. I asked myself that question about a thousand times over whenever I allowed my training get on top of me.

When watching others around you, you can often identify various types of people taking on this challenge. Some have to be in control of every aspect possible. They know to the metre how much they have swum in a season; they can also tell you exactly what they are eating, many can tell you the times that they trained, when and where and some can even tell you their heart rate, when it peaked, and at what point in time it was elevated. Then there are the others who are not too fazed about heart rates, nutrition, charting their swimming or any of that malarkey; the people who just turn up at the training sessions, do exactly what they are told to do and eat what they are given by the team on the beach/shore that has agreed to feed them on their training swim. Depending on who you are and what type of person you are, neither of these is right or wrong. Some people like the detail and others just do exactly what needs to be done to get the job done. With all the different people that take on this challenge, our chances are all exactly the same. We all have a 50/50 chance of being successful or not. The approach taken differs greatly from athlete to athlete and should be unique to you.

I fit into the latter group where I am not too concerned with details at all, only the journey that I am on and the end goal. For me, getting bogged down in detail uses up valuable time when I could be focusing on other important areas of my training. I could not tell you how much I trained in a week. I have and still have no idea what my heart rate is at peak or rest. I do not know my blood type. I eat exactly what I want to, when I want to. I do not have any focus on my nutrition apart from what I have learnt by just doing exactly what I was told from the group that I used to train with. I do little land-based strength training, I just swim. Apart from Pilates to keep my core strength up and focus on my breathing and relaxation, I do not do any other form of training.

Reiterating what I am trying to portray throughout this whole book: Does my way work? Yes – for me. Do the other ways work? Yes - for countless people who have used that approach and technique and managed to get through. Will my approach or someone else's approach work for you? Probably not. We are all individuals and our circumstances, outlook, time availability is all unique to us, and our adopted training regime must fit in with your life, not at the cost of your life, family, work and many other factors.

The one thing I like to do with people that I coach is to get a break down of their week. Now I do not have any children yet, so my circumstances are very different from others out there, but I do a very simple breakdown with people:

There are 168 hours in the week.

Now, minus the following:

Work	- 40 hours (if you are lucky)
Travel	- 10 hours (based on 2 hours a day)
Sleep	- 49 hours (based on 7 hours per night)
Ablutions	- 3.5 hours (30 min per day)
Food preparation	- 7 hour (1 hour per day)
Cleaning	-7 hours (1 hour per day)
Ironing	- 2 hours
Gardening	- 3 hours per week
TV/social media	- 14 hours (2 hours per day)
Social time	- 4 hours per week

In MY life, I only have 28.5 hours left over. In what is left, I need to dedicate time to my wife and family, my training, my Pilates, running a side-line business, managing my website and keeping up with extended family and friends. Recently, a few of those months have also had to include moving my whole house into storage and house hunting on some Saturdays - sometimes viewing seven houses in a day.

The above is just an overview of my life. Now for those who do have children, throw in making time for their lives, and you will see that time is a commodity in very short supply. From this you will see that a training schedule needs to be adapted for you and this has to be done while taking into account your life circumstances. I am very lucky that I live quite close to my offices and I have to drive past the pool at the gym every day on my way home. For me this is a crucial decision as to where my gym pool is. I know myself and I train nearly always in the evening on the way home, as if I had to get home before I went training, then training would not and often still does not, get done.

One thing I cannot stress more, though - if you are venturing into this game for the first time, you need to do the work. There is no shortcut to get the training in and there is no shortcut to building your way up to 4, 6 or 8 hours in the water or in the gym. When you are doing this, if you are lucky enough to be able to be doing it with an experienced group, listen to the people who organise it and do what they say. There is no point in taking shortcuts; the only person that you will be short-changing is yourself. Once you have a few challenges under your belt, then you can start experimenting, and I do just that with all my swims. I change most aspects of my approach to a goal, including my stroke. By doing this you can learn so much more about yourself and taking yourself out of your comfort zone is one of the very many keys to mastering who you are as a person.

During these times, you will gain a huge insight into yourself and who you are. What keeps your focus? What keeps you getting back in after each feed? How do you overcome the monotony of ploughing through 6- to 8-hour training sets? Starting from very early on, each little milestone is huge and the emotional relief or sense of achievement that you get from tackling each goal along the way is amazing. You will often find people coming out after two hours in tears. It is possibly the longest they have ever done and the emotion on their faces shows. With each goal, emotions will be high. Some can take the emotional rollercoaster in their stride but for others it can be a lot to deal with.

The emotions that you will go through when achieving the little goals will teach you a lot about yourself and your ability to go way out of your comfort zone. A very real part of doing anything outside of your comfort zone is that your mind will impose limits on you. This is totally normal and is the body's way of protecting itself. What you will learn with these events is that your mind will set those limits pretty low. Once you break through those barriers you can then start to see what we are *actually capable of* rather than *what we think we are capable of*. An example of this is the classic "hitting the wall" in any of these events. Most of us will experience this to a certain extent and that is the mentally imposed limit that our mind has set for us. In reality, if you are able to summon up the strength of mind, you can surpass any of those to a huge extent. The key is how to get over that wall and move past it and on to the next limit that you impose on yourself. In some cases, you may hit multiple of these proverbial walls when undertaking a big challenge.

Interestingly, over my 10-year career I have managed to hit many of these walls. There are two which stand out in my mind. The first one I hit was when I was swimming the English Channel. The surprising thing was that it was about thirty minutes after the longest swim I had ever done, which was an 8-hour training stint that had been done with some grumbling. While out in the Channel, at about 8 hours 30 minutes, I broke down - just stopped swimming and cried into my goggles for a while and figured that I was done, it was all over. The surprising thing is how soon it came after my longest swim time. After stopping the boat and my team trying to get me to carry on by inching away from me whenever I approached the boat and me having a swearing match with my brother, I figured that they were not going to let me on the boat so I had better carry on. The question that I had asked myself a thousand times was asked at least another hundred times in this episode before I carried on.

The second notable time when I hit a brick wall was my most recent swim in Loch Lomond, where the water temperature averages between 13 and 14°C. As I mentioned previously, Roger Hamilton, an experienced coach, had joined my support crew on the boat at the last minute. I also hired my boat from him. He was not meant to be there, as I had only hired the boat and not his time. As it turns out I am very glad he was onboard with us. Even though I was confident about swimming in that temperature, the entire swim was to be done at night and things got pretty ugly very early on. For me as the swimmer I was confident that all I needed to do was jump in and hammer out the first two hours to generate the body heat I needed to keep warm. At my two-hour feed I had not generated that heat, so I swam another hour pretty swiftly, much faster than I was planning on. At the three-hour feed I was in tears and I mentioned to my team that I was frozen. The cold water was sapping both my energy and my will to carry on. Alarm bells also started ringing with my support crew, as I have never felt the cold to the extent of complaining about it. I broke down, I felt disorientated, and began hyperventilating, nearly in tears. I so desperately wanted to just give up. Not only was I physically in a very dark place, but my mind was plumbing new depths of its own. It was possibly the lowest point I have ever been to in my mind during a swim. I did not realise it but I was experiencing the beginnings of hypothermia! I stopped and surveyed the scene around me, the entire 360 degrees, constantly mumbling, "where is my boat, where is my boat?" I began to panic - I was now without a support boat. In reality, the boat was about three metres away from me but amongst my tears, disorientation and hallucinations, I just couldn't see my boat and support crew. I was handed a warm feed and all I heard was Roger and my team shouting, "Keep calm! Get your breathing under control". It took me about 5 minutes to calm my breathing. I told my team I wanted to get out. This was not going to happen, they said, just another half an hour and then we will see. From then on, my entire feeding plan was shelved, and I received hot feeds on ALL my feeds, which were upped in frequency from hourly to every thirty minutes. I also had to adjust my technique. One of my goggles was leaking slightly, and I swam pretty much with my eyes closed, only opening them every 20 – 30 strokes to make sure I could see the boat. This had the added benefit of effectively removing all forms of sensory input so that I could focus entirely on keeping warm and inwardly on managing my body and my stroke. After about eight hours, the panic was over as I started threatening to punch Robert. I was sick and tired of him and my team just telling me to put my head down and swim – another 30 min – another 30 min- another 30 min, etc., etc. The tough love and the change in my feeding regime were what turned certain failure into another successful swim. By tough love, I mean here that some people just need to have their backsides kicked every so often and this is where Robert did an amazing job. Had it just been the Slimhippo and the Pygmy hippo, who only really had a rudimentary understanding of the effects of hypothermia, and no irritating Glaswegian, I honestly would have got out after about 3 hours.

When training for endurance events, you will often be on your own. Quite understandable really. Unless you are fortunate to live very close to someone who has a similar goal in mind, there are not that many people out there who will be happy to join you for a six to eight-hour swim. They may of course join you for bits of it, which can break up the monotony of a long training set. If you are part of an organised training unit that trains for an hour at a time, use that time as either a warmup or cool down to a much longer set. Either start with them and then go into your own training sets. Or, vice versa.

For those who do not have a lake, river or ocean on their doorstep, or are just training all year in a climate that forces you indoors or into a public pool for half the year, keep things varied! If you are training in a pool, 3 hours non-stop swimming can be mind-numbing. An alternative approach would be to mix things up the whole time, such as by doing sets rather than huge long swims. There are a few concepts that can help with keeping things varied on long training swims in the pool, but before that another important habit to get into is not to chase your watch (times). For years I trained without a watch and just used the clocks on the poolside. Then one year I decided to get one of the smartwatches … sadly, it became my god in the pool. Constantly trying to monitor my times and then pore over the results, it was not very long before chasing times became more important than swimming. My drill work also almost totally dried up. I now do not use my watch EVERY time I am in the pool and this leaves me free to swim and actually get back to the reason I am there - the enjoyment! Chasing times took that away from me. In other words, technology and aids can be very useful but can also hinder your progress if you let them.

During nearly all my pool based training, there are 4 concepts that I rely on and they are:

- Total body confusion
- Negative splitting
- Active rest
- High intensity vs high Mileage

Let's look at these individually.

Total Body Confusion

This entails arriving at poolside with no set already written down and ready to follow. Often making your training sets up on the fly can be very useful. How does this work? Let's say you are planning on doing 8km in the pool. There are countless ways in which you can tackle this (8 x1000m springs to mind), but here is an example of mixing it up and constantly switching between distance, sprints and rest time.

Based on a 25m pool:

Warm up 500m either as a straight swim or every 4th length switch strokes

500m done as 5 x 100m (race pace)

10 x 200m sprint pace with 15 seconds rest between them

1000m easy swim alternating breathing patterns as follows:

- 1st length – breathe every 3 strokes
- 2nd length – breathe every 5 strokes
- 3rd length – breathe every 7 strokes.
- 4th length- breathe every 9 strokes.

Repeat pattern for the whole 1000m.

6 x 500m starting slow and shaving 2 – 4 seconds off every one (negative splits) – 15 second rest in between.

12 x 50m sprints

500m warm down

In the above set we worked on pace keeping, breathing and sprinting.

There are times when I can just arrive at the pool and swim 8km non-stop or I can do the whole lot as a pyramid set. Getting longer and longer to a point, then back down.

Active rest

Let's take the above set. Now you will swim all of that non-stop, BUT, where there is a rest period, you switch strokes and put in a length of very easy swimming where you can get your breath back. For instance, if your main training is using the freestyle, for your rest, use breaststroke. The emphasis on these lengths of breaststroke is REST, so you are ready for the next part of your set.

This will get you used to the idea of not stopping and just carrying on with your training with no rest at the ends of the pool. It can also help imprinting on your mind and body the idea of switching it up a gear when you need to. This is often necessary in ocean swims or if you are racing. Often towards the end of a Channel swim, you may be asked to up your pace to be able to combat the tides to land a swim. Now upping the pace when you have been swimming for 14 - 16 hours can be the last thing you want to do - but can be the difference between either a successful swim and an unsuccessful one, or missing a point and having to swim for another 4 – 6 hours. Being able to switch your pace can be a very useful tool to have in your arsenal.

You could also use one armed breaststroke or backstroke for your rest stroke. You might find this really odd. The reason to do this is that this way of swimming is very common when you are feeding on most long swims. In the channel, with the tides that are running it is not advisable to stop and tread water when you take on feeds. The reason for this is that the moment you stop, it does not mean the tide does. Whilst you are treading water, you could very well be being washed back in the direction you have just come, or at least being affected in a negative fashion by the tide. For this reason, one armed breaststroke or any stroke that helps you to maintain some momentum is crucial. For example, if a tide is running at 6 knots (11.16km/hour) while you are treading water, the tide will move you about 200m in a minute. So, if you are on a predicted 15-hour swim, feeding for 1 minute every hour, that is 14 minutes' worth of feeding and you could lose 200m every minute you are stationary. That equates to 2800m that you would have lost due to treading water! Feeding when on the move is a handy thing to be able to do. In the Marathon swims of the Olympics, most athletes just grab a cup of feed, roll onto their back for a stroke or two of backstroke before rolling onto their fronts to continue the race. Done properly, this can save crucial seconds in a marathon type race.

Negative splits

Take a very simple set of 500m warmup, 14 x 500m and 500m cooldown. The idea here is to start really slowly and progressively get faster with each 500m. To do this for all 14 of them requires you to have a good knowledge of your pace. If you go out fast on the first one, then getting faster is going to really challenge you, so start of at your "swim forever pace" then slowly crank up the speed until your 14th 500m is about 30 – 40 seconds faster. Now, if you are planning on 100 x 100m it goes without saying that you are not going to keep increasing the speed on every 100m. So, a way to tackle this set is to do 5 x 100m at 120 seconds, 5 at 100 seconds, and 5 at 90 seconds and repeat this six times.
I gauge my endurance on how many sets I can negative split, and over time, I increase that number of sets.

This is a very good way to learn to adjust your pace as well as test your endurance along the way. If you are getting this right, you will find that in the longer distance races that you take part in, you will get faster as the race goes further.

I talk about races as this is another good way to mix things up and get you out of the pool and into a more competitive environment. The smaller races that I take part in are generally 3 or 5km races after work at my local lake. They are predominantly frequented by triathlete and pool swimmers who are getting in a bit of open water experience. The starts can be frantic, especially with racing triathletes, as they generally sprint off at the start. I on the other hand am not a sprinter and I get into my comfortable stroke very quickly and then spend the rest of the race catching up swimmers in front of me. What usually happens is that they blow themselves out after about 500m to 1km (the point where I am just getting into my race) and when I am racing those distances, it is very common for me to be able to increase my speed the further I go. If and when it comes to a sprint finish, I find that I have lots left in the tank and can push my speed way up in the last 500m. You can see how training with a negative split as much as you can is very useful.

A fourth option when you doing the really long sets, is to adopt all of the three concepts and throw them into your training set. Total body confusion, active rest and negative splits. This will give you a good overall workout for distance, sprinting, technique training and breathing tests.

With all of this physical training, it is a very good time to learn what your capabilities are by revisiting the base tests you did in the early part of your training in the pool. These are timed sets at varying effort, so you know what to start at when you are, for instance, doing negative splits. You do not want to start off too fast if you know you are only wanting to get quicker the whole time. It is also an opportunity to see if you have become faster with the training.

To mix things up a bit and if you are just using the splits technique, you could swing both ways, a bit like a pyramid but instead of using distances, use times. Negative split for five sets then positive split (getting slower) for five, go up and down as many times as you feel is necessary. Whilst the Holy

Grail for nearly all of us is to swim faster, it is also a very good thing to be able to swim slowly. I find that the slower my cadence is, the faster I go as, as I am spending more time concentrating on making every stroke the best it can be. If I sprint, I am generally so busy breathing to keep my lungs full of air, that I stop concentrating on my stroke and the result is a slower swim, as there is absolutely no way that I can keep up the effort except over short distances.

For most of the above we are talking about pool distances, as it is easy to do all the monitoring and the likes in the pool where conditions remain constant. Once the open water season opens, you will then be in the rivers, lakes and oceans and your training will then change from distance in the water to time in the water. At the beginning of the season you may be doing 30 minute dips a few times a day. This is due to the water temperatures being too cold to do long distance. As the summer wears on, you will slowly increase the time you spend in the water where the conditions will change from day to day, so it becomes very difficult to monitor pace, speed and estimated time to swim a specific distance.

In my last swim, if I extrapolated my times over 10km (2 hrs 20 min – or just over 4.1km per hour), then in my big swim of the season of 34.5km, it stood to reason that I could do it in 8.5 hours. Take into account feeding, and the likes, I guessed between 9 and 10 hours. Oh, how wrong I was. I obviously had not taken into account the effects of hypothermia and generally wasting FAR too much time at my numerous feeds. It finally took me 11.5 hours – an average speed of

3km/hour. To say I was disappointed was an understatement. It just goes to prove that there are a lot of factors that can affect your overall speed. No two open water swims are the same - throw in more factors and then there is a greater propensity to slow down. It just goes to prove, unless you are very fast, do not ever go into ultra-distance challenges with a time in mind, as there are way too many factors beyond your control and a lot more time for things to go wrong.

Even in open water you can still adopt total body confusion. You can work on swimming longer and longer without breathing and you can work on your bilateral breathing. This is not essential in swimming but can be a very useful tool to have when it comes to the rough stuff. You can also mix it up in many other ways as usually, your rest periods will be when you decide to take on food. Commonly, people feed either half hourly, hourly and sometimes longer when in open water.

High intensity vs High Mileage

This addresses the question of what is more beneficial in training for a distance event. Is it better to swim shorter distances at a very high intensity, or is it better to get the mileage in? In my opinion, I think that if this is the first big event that you are doing, you need to do the mileage. This is not only to get your muscle memory built up, but more importantly to train your mind. Nothing is going to prepare you to 'hit the wall' unless you have hit those walls before in training. You will learn what happens when your mind does start to have a meltdown and then learn how to deal with it when it does. As you stay longer and longer in the water, that barrier will soon become a familiar episode and the techniques that you've developed to deal with that wall will become well practiced until you can easily get past it. YOU NEED TO DO THE TIME TO LEARN THIS.

Once you have a few hefty swims under your belt or when you are in the pool leading up to the open water season, you can experiment. I learnt this when I happened to train with someone in the pool who was aiming for the same long-distance goal. I would never train and still never train more than 1.5 to 2 hours in a pool set. I adopted the high intensity route, with the whole set done using the three aforementioned techniques – TBC, negative splits and active rest. I always made sure that at the end of my 2 hours I had done anything between 8 and 9km, while the person who was with me often achieved about 5 -6km in the same time. The difference - I was absolutely knackered at the end of my sets while they had barely raised their heart rate at all. I could barely drag myself out of the pool when they leapt out as if they had just done a short swim. They were doing the time in the water, but their intensity was a lot less than mine was.

To really get my heart rate going, I used to train every now and then with the water polo team - their sets were very short, their biggest swim in a set being 100m, but it was done at a phenomenal pace. I could barely hold on to their toes!

Sessions very rarely went over 2.5km but they were done at a very fast speed with very little rest between the sets, with the objective being training for quick bursts of speed rather than long drawn out swims. This all went towards the mixing up of my training. It also gave me the confidence that if I needed to pick the pace up at any point, I could.

Although I mostly used the high intensity route, I do believe that "garbage yardage", as it is often referred to, is a useful thing to do. Even if it is just another way of changing things up! Very occasionally I would just jump in and swim with absolutely no plan in mind, just to get the distance in at a fairly easy pace. This also helped with the boredom, by **not** having a set in mind, **not** breaking up the swim, **not** altering tempo and just swimming 160 - 200 lengths. Sets can be very useful but they do take up a lot of concentration to keep on track, even if it is trying to remember how many lengths you have done. If, like me, you struggle to count past about four lengths, you start questioning yourself as to how many lengths you have done. There is often a lot of arithmetic going on in my head during a training set. So just swimming with nothing to think about, apart from my stroke and how efficient I can make it, keeps it simple.

In the ten years I have been doing ultra-distance, I have experimented with all my swims. For the English Channel I did the distance and also did many 6- to 8-hour swims. It was the first big swim I had ever taken on. With all that time invested into it, I was keen to do the preparation that was needed to maximise my chances of succeeding. A few years later, for a 28km lake swim in Lago D'Orta, I tried a different route. I kept every training swim under 90 minutes. I wanted to test a theory that short regular swims could be used as training for a long swim, so I swam four times per week, but never more than ninety minutes - sometimes less. I then took on this 28km challenge and the results were surprising. After 4 hours of swimming with the leading three swimmers, I stopped for a feed. The other two left me and I fed quickly, but I could not get the distance I had lost back and I had the most spectacular mental meltdown after about 5 hours. The Slimhippo was on the end of possibly the worst side of me whilst I threw all my toys out of my cot. There was a storm around that day and I so desperately wanted the organisers to abandon the swim. I knew I was not going to be the one to abandon it willingly, but I so desperately wanted that call to happen to get me out of this torture I was in. After 6 hours I settled down after verbally abusing my support crew to carry on and finish in 8 hours. I think it was as much a lesson for her as it was for me. The Slimhippo had never seen this side of me and was ill-prepared on how to deal with it, but she as usual was amazing and managed to calm me down and get my mind back into the task at hand. The result was that I finished, and I did manage to get on the podium, but I really did not deserve to be there and would not advocate that approach as a sole form of training. If anything, the one thing that I would have loved to have been able to do was to find out how much that meltdown affected my time. I reckon that between 1 and 3 hours I was cruising at about 4.2km/hr. Between 3 and 6 hours I would easily say that my time dropped to well below 3km/hr in amongst all the whining and bitching. Between 6 and 8 hours, I reckon that I was back up to or very near 4.0km/hour. I would say that I should have been somewhere between 6.5 – 7 hours for that swim but my mind had let me down badly.

Then for Loch Lomond I did a mixture of both, a few long swims but mostly 2- to 4-hour swims. The results were even worse; after a mere 3 hours I was moving towards hypothermia and every fibre in my body just wanted to get out. Here it was more down to the quick thinking of my support team recognising that I was going hypothermic and making vital changes, like altering my feeding intervals and type of feed, and a lot of TOUGH LOVE that kept me going to finish in 11.5 hours - again being the fastest on the day, but very well off the pace I had hoped to set. It was by far the coldest swim I had ever done. It was also the hardest swim I have ever done. Lakes are very different to the ocean and have their own set of challenges associated with them. This was a swim that was not accomplished by me, but my team. I have always realised that this sport is not a sport that can be done alone, but this swim was to prove beyond any doubt that a good team is the difference between an unsuccessful swim and a successful one. If it were not for them, I WOULD definitely have given up after 3 hours.

After 11.5 hours overnight in Loch Lomond

In conclusion, the physical training needs to be done - so do as much as you can, bearing in mind that you have a life outside of the water and this all needs to be taken into context with regards your family, work and other life commitments.

Chapter 7: Training your mind

In my colourful past, I have been fortunate enough to attend, organise and then train to be a lecturer in personal development, with the main aim of unlocking more of the mind than we currently use. This is where my passion lies - the mental training. When I started this journey, I was a prime candidate to dust off the techniques I had been taught and put them to the test. To say I was a million miles off mentally prepared for anything remotely like swimming to France, was an understatement. I was down but definitely not out. I had as much chance as anyone who takes on this challenge. It is all 50/50 so it was time to shift that probability to a more positive outcome.

In my opinion, this is my biggest form of training and I really do spend about 60 – 70 % of my overall training sitting quietly, relaxing and training my mind. I am often known as the one who does not train enough for events and in comparison to others out there, I would totally agree. If your idea of training is purely focused on your physical side then yes, I do not train a lot but I prefer to spend my time calmly focusing on mental fortitude. I may only get to the pool or the gym twice a week, and occasionally I may not even get to do any physical training during the week, but when it comes to my mental preparation, this is generally done in one form or another 7 days a week, 365 days a year. I do not need a gym, a pool, a pair of speedos or goggles, all I need is some time during the day to sit down quietly and get to work on my mind.

In the last chapter I posed the theory that an endurance swim is 70 % mental, 20% physical and 10% luck. So let's explore this. If this is true, why do people only spend a tiny fraction on focusing on this aspect of their training? Which, in theory, has a 70% chance of getting you through it?

 The only reason you are at this point in your life is not because of any physical attribute that you might have, it is the result of a thought – a mental thought. Everything you have done in your life is the result of a thought, your mental ability to make these thoughts. Whenever there is a big decision to make, most people want to go away and think about it, not go away and do something extremely physical! If they do, this is generally because they are able to think better while doing something physical. Another comment you might hear people say when they have to make a big decision is "let me sleep on it". Other times that we can make our best decisions are sitting on the loo, relaxing in a bath, (*Archimedes came up with probably his greatest theory whilst lying in a bath) or meditation of some description. Now what do lying in a bath, taking a shower, sitting on the loo and meditation, all have in common? And even the lengthier endurance sports? During any of them, you are in a state of heightened relaxation. This is one of the fundamental states to be in when you want to alter your mental outlook, and it is an ideal state to be in when you are mentally training your mind for anything in life.

Archimedes was possibly the world's greatest scientist — at least the greatest in the classical age. He was a physicist, mathematician, astronomer, inventor and engineer. Many of his inventions, theories and concepts are still in use today. Perhaps his best-known achievement was his "Eureka" moment, when he discovered the principle of buoyancy.

Nowadays you are able to go on plenty of training camps where you will learn about the physical side, the nutritional side of things, the different types of diets used, different techniques for different conditions, get plenty of time in the water, possibly learn about the physiology of long distance swimming from some very accomplished people. The list can go on, all with very good intentions, and the information gleaned from these sessions is invaluable. But I believe you would be hard pressed to find a single word spoken about how you can maximise your chances by preparing your mind correctly.

So why is it that we all opt for the physical side of things and in many cases completely ignore the mental side - after all, that is probably the reason that you are here, reading this book! I think the main reason is that there is no gym you can go to to exercise your brain, there are no recommended ways to exercise your mind. There is no easy way to chart and gauge the results that you can achieve by utilising your mental capabilities. This poses a big problem for people who like to be in control of everything. At least with the physical training, you can chart how many lengths you did, how your times were increasing and decreasing, or what your heart rate at the certain points along your training. You are also able to pretty much chart your nutrition and every aspect about your physical training. All of which, by the way, were initiated by a mental thought.

Unfortunately, there are not many courses out there to be able to maximise the use of our brain. Historically it was believed that, as humans we only use between 10 and 12% of our mental capacity. This myth has been debunked over the years. But the question still remains - how are some people able to achieve so much in their lives whilst, for the rest of us, we struggle with the effort of existing day to day? What differentiates ordinary from extra- ordinary, success from failure?

The whole premise of mental training that I live by is: "What the mind believes the body will achieve." To put it another way, the mind does not know the difference between what is real and what is vividly imagined.

First, let's explore the simplest technique you can employ to help your training.

Speak the right words

Often when I speak to people who plan on taking on a challenge, which will effectively put them way out of their comfort zone, the most common word I hear (and I think the most divisive word) is the word ATTEMPT. Why is this?

Well, if you are going to talk about doing something, by using a word with a negative or defeatist tone, it will only cause your mind to question whether you are going to do it or not. Take the following example:

I am going to attempt to swim to France! (Or any other marathon type event)

OR

I am going to swim to France!

The first sentence, in my opinion, puts you 50% closer to failure as when you say those words, what you mind hears is, that's okay, this is only an *attempt*. If we fail, well, it was only ever an attempt.

The second way of saying it is far more definite. It leaves your mind with no question. This is not just an *attempt*. You are GOING to swim there.

The more and more that you say this in your daily conversations with friends, colleagues and family, or even to yourself , in your head, it is another opportunity to impress upon your mind that you are *going* to swim there. As the thought matures from just being in your head, to verbalising it to others, this cements the idea into your brain as a new program that you are going to follow. If you want that cement to set hard and fast then verbalise it in the most positive way possible. Another way to cement a thought is to write it down on a piece of paper, in a notebook, or on a pad.

Some people will even write it on a poster and place that poster in a very prominent place so it can be seen every day, sometimes multiple times a day. Often people will put the poster where it is the last thing they see when they go to bed and the first thing they see when they open their eyes. The timing of when you see these messages is very important.

So be careful how you speak *to* yourself and *about* yourself. Just by your words alone, you have one of the most powerful mental manipulators known to man. By your words alone you can make or break a goal. Just take a moment to think how your words can affect others around you. You can say something to someone that will totally destroy their world. You can also say something to them that will make them feel great, inspired or elated. If you have that power with words on other people, you also have that power on yourself.

So now that you are constantly talking about your goal or verbalising it in your head – using the correct language - you are bound to come across the naysayers, the doubters and the cynics out there. They may have these attitudes based on very good evidence. Take my very first foray into this sport of open water swimming. If I am going to take something on, I might as well do a good job, so I picked the biggest challenge out there. To say that there were doubters amongst my friends and colleagues was an understatement. I do not blame them. I was loudmouthed, overweight, I drank more than I should have, I never did any exercise and I smoked – effectively, I was a bit of a car wreck waiting to happen. They had good solid evidence that I could be a bit of a charlatan.

Another reason that doubts existed was that for nearly all my friends and family at the time, none of them had ever met anyone who could not afford a ferry trip or plane ticket to France. I had many offers of just that. I was the first person that they knew of that was going to swim the Channel. To them, in their minds, and mine initially, it was something that extraordinary people did - and I was very far from that. With the attitude of "nothing ventured, nothing gained" and" if others have done it, there is no reason I could not do it", I carried on spreading the word that I was going to swim to France, no matter what the responses were.

I was often fobbed off when I spoke about it. I honestly think that there were maybe only a handful of people who actually took me seriously. An example was Mike Bass and his wife Debbie. We had only known each other about a year so they did not really know me very well. When I was attending a get-together, and I started mouthing off about this insane plan that I was going to swim the Channel (with a beer in one hand and a cigarette in the other!), they were asking my longer- term friends if I was actually serious about this or whether it was just a whole lot of rubbish that I was talking. They were not alone. Even my long-term friends were sceptical. None of them knew anyone who had ever undertaken something like this and I was probably the least likely candidate among my friends who would even dream of doing something like this. To say there were very few who actually shared my belief in myself that were 100% behind me and 100% positive in their support for me, was a very true statement.

My advice: - when you have a burning desire, do not let anyone rain on your parade. Listen to the doubters, take their opinions on board but be selective as to which ones you listen to. I say that because over time, those doubters watched my progress from a distance, listened and slowly started to take on my belief in myself. I was unable to join them for parties and gatherings as I was down at the coast swimming, or in a pool or lake training, and soon the tide of scepticism from them started to change. Even when I was standing on the beach about to start, there were people who doubted me. But that tide soon turned into a flood of admiration and eventually they all became an integral part of my positive supporters. Their doubt actually fuelled my desire to complete this even more. That fuel was in the form of playful banter (which in the case of my really good friends can become quite vindictive, especially when they gang up on me). You might ask why I have them as friends, but I would not change it for anything. Having been friends for years I have generally learnt to ignore it but, this habit became a big driving force. Here's how. During the event, when I felt tired and ready to give up, my thoughts turned to my friends. If I did succeed, I might be sore and stiff for a few days but that would go in time. If I did not succeed, the banter and ridicule would be endless for the rest of my life. If I did not want to end up being known as "the guy who nearly swam to France", I knew I had better get on and finish this task. They actually have no idea how much time and effort it takes to just get to the start of an event like this. The preparation, in reality, is the most difficult part. From that point on you are in the hands of the gods, your team, the weather and many other factors. I think my friends are amazing but this is one way in which friendships can drive you. Odd, but it can work!

Now we have a goal, we have verbalised it, and we have our supporters - both the positive and negative ones. It does not matter what guise their support takes, as long as it is there and productive, we are now well on the road. Now we encounter a problem that we all suffer from.

Focus!

Many of you will say "Focus on the goal". This is all well and good and in the real world it is entirely commonplace to do just that. Now, if it is a short goal, then a vast majority of your focus should go on the goal, but for long term goals that are sometimes six months, a year, or in many cases several years, focusing on the goal can be very tedious and counterproductive. You may ask - if we are not focusing on the goal, then what else is there? The answer is to focus on THE JOURNEY. In any goal, this is by far the biggest portion of it. Your goal may last two hours or two days, but the journey to get there will last for a lot longer, and will involve hundreds of little goals along the way, each one just as important if not more so than the ultimate goal.

Taking on a marathon swim will involve your first 2km swim, your first outdoor swim, your first swim in the ocean, your first 5km swim. Moving on to your first two, three, six and probably eight-hour swim. It will also involve meeting important people and gaining knowledge from those in the know. Go ahead. Immerse yourself in each and every one. Experience the emotions that go with each goal and treat them as a goal in their own right. No need to wait for the ultimate one to immerse yourself in and the emotions associated with it.

In my experience, my first goal was to be able to do 4km in the pool. Next was to be able to achieve the same time per 100m as I did at the beginning of my set as they got longer. Being able to negative split my entire training set was the next goal. After that it was my first dip in cold water, then my first dip in saltwater – knowing full well how I hated the taste of saltwater. Once that goal was accomplished, we moved onto the bigger goals. Next goal was my first 2-hour swim in the ocean. Each of these little goals was accompanied by an emotional boost and a growth in my confidence that I was on the right track. I immersed myself in the sensation of achieving these little goals and gave myself a very positive mental "high five" on the realisation that I was getting my mind on track. In no time at all, I was being tasked with a 6-hour swim by the Channel General and her team. This was to be the much-needed 6 hour qualifying swim in water temperatures below 16°C that I had to undertake to be able to progress to the Channel, as part of health and safety requirements. Hearing those words "you are in for 6 hours", a wave of doubt engulfed me. This was a bit of a shock, as it was a great deal more than the 4 hours that I had been tasked with the previous week. The fear of not attaining this goal was a massive weight on my mind. The thoughts that I had previously harboured about me being a charlatan came flooding back with vengeance. A 6-hour swim is no small task. In the interests of mixing it up to keep the boredom at bay, my friend and training partner then decided to be adventurous and after three hours of swimming we tried a sprint leg of the harbour in Dover (okay sprint in this case is a relative term). In those days, the distance across the harbour was about 1400m. Try that with full after burners after three hours of being rinsed in the harbour waves! After that we still had about 2 hours and 40 minutes left to go! You did not even think about getting out before 6 hours was up, as the General would only haul your ass back in to complete the 6 hours. This goal was the one which produced the most emotion and I just broke down and cried when I finally got to the end of it. The next goal was a night-time swim; this brought about another emotional outburst. A group of us gathered down at the beach after a pretty hefty day's training, and after sunset, we went in for a two-hour swim before it was time to head off to bed - only to do it all again in about seven hours later.

Even when it comes to an eight-hour training swim, break down the hours into little goals and mix it up as much as possible. With each length of the harbour, I used it as a fun time to adjust my stroke and play with new ideas, different breathing patterns, different speeds, drafting, etc. The overall goal for these big swims was, SWIM TILL MY NEXT FEED. Rewards were simple things like jelly babies, chocolate at the end of each hour with my energy drink, and the ultimate goal for the day was several burgers and chips at the end and a really long hot bath.

The key here is to break down your goals into manageable chunks and live through the experience. Let yourself enjoy them and reward yourself for each goal. The main reason why we break up a goal of this magnitude is to give our minds time to adapt to the new program that we are trying to build it towards. Our minds generally do not cope well with big goals like "I am going to swim 6 hours", so we break it down. In essence we are slowly reprogramming our minds and, as with any computer programme written out there, it is only as good as the code base it was built on. If that is not stable, then the software suffers. In computers it is easy to fix, you either kick it or reboot it, and worst case is you recode the software. It's a little bit harder to reboot a living breathing entity. Changing the course of your life needs many things to take place but most importantly, be firm and sure with what you set out to do.

Our minds like small bite size challenges. Even when you have done all the work and you standing on the banks/shore/start line ready to swim to a point somewhere out there (that you cannot even see!), your mind will freak out as the magnitude of the task is just too big for meaningful comprehension. So give it manageable goals to aim for. If you give it a goal that is too big to understand of course it is not going to be happy to agree to that (I don't think anyone would agree to do something with such vague instructions, unless they were absolutely bonkers or ill-informed) so swim until the next feed and do not stop until the final destination.

The above assumes that all your goals are met throughout the journey. This is not often the case. Some may call it failure. I disagree. Failure is just a term that humans have invented that has huge negative connotations. How we deal with "not being successful" is very important. Along the journey, everything we do is building on past experiences. With all of those there is a psychological and emotional response. There is very little point in dwelling on them and beating yourself up about it. Remember, the aim is to keep it positive. Treat all little goals as good training along the way. Be aware of your reactions and if you do happen to come up short, that is fine. The worst thing that you can do if this happens is ask the fatal question – "what if................?" The list is endless. By all means dissect the situation and take what you can from the experience, but every moment you spend dissecting an area where you were not up to the task robs you of a moment when you could be spending valuable mind power focusing on the next. Learn from the episode and move on, you cannot change anything by dwelling in the past but you can alter the future as long as you choose to live in the now.

Mantras

The next area that can be of enormous benefit are what some people call mantras. Basically, mundane sentences packed with positive connotations, which are repeated over and over and over. The entire way we learn throughout life is by repetition. How we learn languages, how we learn maths, how we learn to speak, pretty much everything we have become good at has involved some level of repetition. If these mantras are said when you are in a calm relaxed environment, it is like you are tapping into your subconscious brain and inputting a new reality.

Common mantras that I use and have known others to use are:

"Every day in every way I am more and more successful."

"Every day, in every way I get happier, healthier and fitter."

"One arm in front of the other until you reach the end."

"Just keep swimming, just keep swimming, and just keep swimming."

So how did they help me? These were often utilised when I was going to bed at night. I used to close my eyes and then say one of my mantras over and over and over again, believing the whole time that I would at some point be entering into the mind state where I was most susceptible to making a change in my life. Let's take my most common saying: "Every day in every way I am healthier, happier and fitter."

Saying a mantra forces the mind to take a time out and concentrate on just one thing. You do not have to physically speak them out loud (fortunately for the Slimhippo) - just say them in your mind. I pretty much guarantee that you will not be able to close your eyes and say any of these mantras in your head for more than a minute without some other thoughts invading your thought processes. So saying these mantras serves two purposes – we talk to ourselves in a very positive and highly influential way and learn to master the ability to focus. What we are focusing on here is the ability to totally calm the mind and declutter it of any thoughts which might not be useful, or worse still – NEGATIVE. Typically what happens is when you start saying one of these mantras, your brain, believing them to be totally mundane, starts you thinking about something else to get away from the monotony - maybe that email you forgot to send, the phone call you forgot to make, the shopping you did not pick up, the meeting you have tomorrow. However, over time, being able to concentrate on these mantras will become easier and easier, and by simultaneously slowing our brain state down and relaxing, it allows us to access the most powerful part of our minds.

In this day and age, where we have possibly the greatest ability to succeed and make a huge difference in our wellbeing, we are simultaneously living in a world where we WANT everything, and we live our lives accordingly. We want the big house, the big family, the amazing job, great health, great friendships, the perfect body, and the great children, to achieve all our goals, to excel in everything we do. The reality is very different. Be aware that when you spend more time focusing on one, that time is taken away from something else. We cannot be EVERYTHING TO EVERYONE, but we can be the best us that we can.

With the internet and our instant access to information and other people's achievements, as I have mentioned earlier, one of the biggest pitfalls I have seen is that it's easy to compare ourselves to others out there. When we log in and read blogs about people's training, how far and fast they have gone, and marvel at these "photoshopped lives" out there, we don't always understand how their achievements came about. The hardships, the downfalls, the failures and the time and effort that has taken to get to that very point are rarely if ever mentioned. Doubt and despondency is inevitable and it can be a struggle to remain focused.

You might say that it drives us to push ourselves further and harder. But one thing you have not considered is ability. Take a 6-hour qualifying swim for the English Channel (bear in mind that the record is just under 7 hours). For the fastest out there, if they trained six hours on Saturday and six hours on Sunday, they would have effectively crossed the channel in both training sets. At the other end of the scale, that is barely 20% of the distance. Some can comfortably swim at 4.5 – 5km/hour whilst others are more comfortable at 2 km/hour. Do the fastest and the slowest require the same time in the water for training? The answer is no. The best thing you can do is to STOP comparing yourself to others and START being the best YOU can be. Most of these challenges are NOT against a human opponent; they are challenges against yourself and the elements. So, don't train to somebody else's training plan, build your own. If that requires the intervention of a coach, then get one on board to help you build your plan and customise it for you.

Other good times to use the mantras are when you wake up in the morning, before you get out of bed, sitting in a bath, sitting on the loo, or when you are relaxing on the train on your way to work. One thing that all the above scenarios have in common is that it is a time when we are taking a break from the day, our minds are slowing down and relaxing and this is a great time to be able to start to try to reprogram your mind.

You might very well ask - how is this going to help? I am not going to guarantee that it is, but if you have time to do the mantras, you have a 50% chance that they will be effective at helping you prepare for a challenge, and I would rather take those odds and use the time to at least try and make the difference rather than not use them. What have you got to lose? An important thing to have here is the belief that you are making a difference. Remember, our minds cannot tell the difference between what is real and what is imagined.

As adults, our minds are very active, and we can really struggle to focus on one thing entirely for a good length of time. If your work is anything like mine, I can be immersed in a problem one moment and then another call comes in and I am catapulted into another completely different problem, having to put the original issue temporarily on hold. This can culminate in me having to juggle four or five completely different, unrelated issues all at once. Work-life balance becomes a real burden. Most adults are juggling many things at once and the ability to focus on one thing is strongly challenged. Another reason that adults are less capable of learning new things is because we spend the vast majority of the day in a very active mental state, commonly known as Beta. From when we are born to when we are in our middle teens, we are totally unshackled by the burdens of life. We may spend a lot more time sleeping, but as we get older, we spend more and more of our waking days in a different mental state. As children we spend a vast portion of our life in a brain level called Alpha. I am certain that all will agree how easy it is to learn things when you are younger - you are able to concentrate for longer and you absorb things around you at a much faster pace. In most cases you do not have the worries and anxieties that take hold when you grow up. You do not have to worry about mortgage repayments, work stress, not being accepted by people - those only tend to become ingrained as we progress through life.

Chapter 8: What happens in our minds?

At this junction, it is essential to give you a rundown, and hopefully some understanding, of our different mental levels. Throughout the day and at night, we do not get into any single level and stay there but rather cycle through our different brain levels. These brain levels are based on electrical cycles per second or frequency. Our brains operate anywhere between 0 and 45Hz. Science has studied these brain levels – or states – and all these states are vitally important to us as humans. The "states" of mind are directly related to their frequency and are categorised as follows: Beta, Alpha, Theta, Delta and the now lesser known frequency called Gamma.

Beta (12-30Hz) – this is associated with normal waking consciousness, heightened alertness, logical and critical reasoning. Here you can also experience higher levels of stress, anxiety and restlessness. As adults spend most their working day in this level, it is little wonder that we experience stress. It is a fast-growing epidemic in the modern world, with us all trying to manage way too much. While in this level, our neurons are firing at an incredible rate whilst trying to manage all that is being thrown our way.

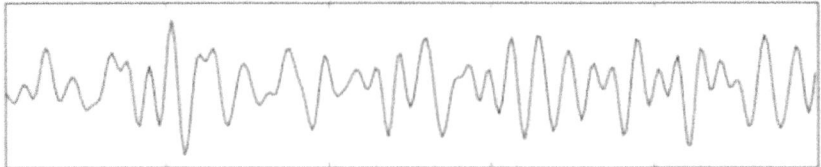

Beta: 12-30 Hz

Alpha (8 -12Hz) – this is associated with deep relaxation with the eyes generally closed and whilst daydreaming. Often this state is achieved through light meditation and is characterised as the best level for programming your mind for success. Often associated with heightened imagination, visualisation, memory, learning and concentration. It is at the lowest level of our conscious awareness and the doorway to our subconscious brain levels. The closer you get to 7.5Hz, the more that intuition starts to become engaged.

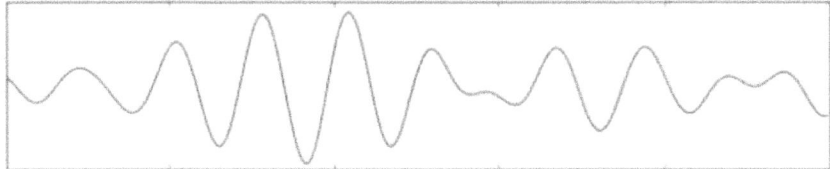

Alpha: 8-12 Hz

Theta (4 – 7.5Hz) Associated with deep meditation and light sleep where REM (Rapid Eye Movement), occurring when we are in our dream state. This is the subconscious mind and is only achieved momentarily when you drift off to sleep and when you start to wake up. It is sometimes known as the spiritual level. An important level, as here we have profound creativity, greater insight and access to the mind's most deep-seated programs.

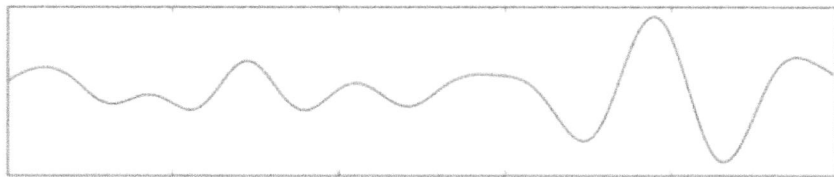

Theta: 4-7 Hz

Delta (0.5 – 4Hz) – The slowest state; this is where we experience deep, dreamless sleep. In this state we can experience transcendental meditation where our awareness is completely detached and we enter into our unconscious state. It is often associated with deep healing and regeneration. It is where our bodies effectively fix themselves.

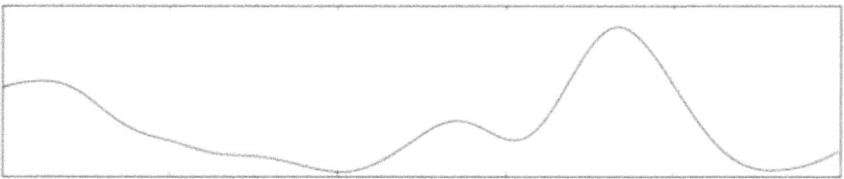

Delta: 0-4 Hz

Understanding these levels is the key to being able to programme ourselves and input new programs into our conscious mind. The best place to do this is at the Alpha-Theta border. During the day these cycles are dictated by how relaxed we are. It is during the day that we spend more time in Alpha and Beta than we do in Theta and Delta. More importantly, as children, we spend more time in Alpha than we do in Beta. As our lives progress, we spend more time in Beta than in Alpha, but we still cycle through these states regularly during the day. Let's take your typical day. You wake up out of Theta and start moving into Alpha - it feels surreal, and you are in a dream state. Then you have to get out of bed and go for a shower and ablutions; you are still at low levels of Alpha and moving on up the scale to Beta. Then on to the commute, and as you have to start planning, think logically, check the roads or transport for foul ups etc, you move up the level closer to Beta. Get to work, where planning, meetings, clients, mail to open, work colleagues to engage with, make appointments, etc., dominates – you reach and stay in the Beta state. Stress levels are elevated, anxieties are more prevalent, and you worry more.

If you then go for a walk, take a time out, sit in the park at lunch or go to the loo, your brain slows down and enters that Alpha state again. Then back to the grindstone, brain frequency increases, and it's back up to Beta again. Then the day ends, you shut down the computer, see the last client, shut the office and the mind starts winding down. You might sit on the train and daydream (not a good idea if driving!), close your eyes and take a cat nap. Brain levels constantly slow.

Then home! Back to Beta for a bit. Time to go to the gym, get that training in, prepare dinner, open up the post, read our emails, get kids ready for bed, tidy the house, put a wash on, hang up the washing that has been in the dryer for the last 3 days, prepare for that meeting tomorrow. Finally the end of the day comes; all chores are done; you maybe have a nice bath, get into bed, read a book – NOT SOCIAL MEDIA OR WORK EMAILS. Our brain waves slow all the time until we drift off.

During the night, upon closing our eyes, we drift into low Alpha and then on into Theta, and experience dreaming and REM. This lasts for a few minutes as we drift deeper and deeper into sleep and reach Delta state, where our bodies are now at their optimum state to heal themselves, regenerate and repair. We experience rhythmic breathing and limited muscle activity. It is very difficult to wake someone from this state. If you have kids, in this level, you can often get them to walk to their bed with assistance but they do not wake up as such and will not even remember it. Once we reach deep sleep/unconsciousness, our brains can then cycle back up into Theta and we may dream again. We could cycle up to the border of Alpha and Theta but as we are not waking up, our brains slow again. Each sleep cycle can last up to 90 minutes as we drift in and out of these different states of mind.

You will all agree that sleep is vital to us. Some are happy with 4 -5 hours and others are much better on 7 – 8 hours, but either way it is pretty crucial. You will also all agree that children are far superior to adults when it comes to learning and picking up new skills. I have heard it said that people are born perfect - it takes life (and adults) to mess them up. This is because children spend most of their day in Alpha. As we get older and spend more and more time in Beta in this logical planning level, we are dedicating very little time for our mind to focus, reprogram, relax and make huge changes.

All these levels serve a purpose, but clearly some levels are more beneficial to us to help get certain things done. We get into all the brain levels every day, mostly without even knowing it, as they are related to how relaxed we are, and we are constantly cycling up and down through these levels all the time, every day of our lives. *But how do we reach the levels we want, when we want?*

Knowing EXACTLY what state of mind you are in is very difficult – unless you have an EEG (Electroencephalograph) machine in your bedroom. Last time I looked, they did not stock them in on the high street. But it goes without saying that the more time we spend in a relaxed state, the slower our brain waves are. Recently, there is a buzzword about town - "Mindfulness". In my opinion, this is just another name for adopting a way of life in which we enforce time for relaxation. Ways to do this are vast and varied. Some are done without any assistance and others employ aids such as, for example, electronic music designed to slow your brain down.

The most common habit employed to help ourselves relax are breathing techniques, which are frequently used in forms of exercise like Pilates, Yoga and other holistic exercises. Part of the exercise is to concentrate on and consciously slow your breathing patterns down, which helps you to focus on the position or exercise ahead. Meditation is another form of slowing your brain down which again gets you to focus on breathing and take control of your body rhythms. Another tip for being able to relax is to close your eyes, which eliminates the stimuli received from our faculty of sight. Even putting headphones on and listening to calm mellow music helps in slowing our brain down.

Manipulating your breathing in endurance sports is vitally important. With my coaching hat on, I believe that breathing comfortably while in the water or exercising is a vital part of being able to exercise for extended lengths of time or take part in the fast-growing sport of ice swimming. To overcome the initial shock of the cold water, it is essential to get your breathing under control. For me, the Holy Grail for endurance swimming is to get your breathing patterns correct. Your breathing should not be laboured in any way, but calm and controlled. This in turn will have the effect of calming your mind. The other benefit of focusing on breathing techniques is that, whilst we are focusing on them, our mind is busy and unable to let the darker side of our minds come to the fore, where the doubts, low self-esteem and many other negative and divisive thoughts take up residence. You can get into a trance like state where everything else around you disappears into the back of your mind.

At this point, let me throw in some real world experience. My mental preparation for my bigger swims involved many of the above techniques to get to my optimum point of preparation. I still use nearly all these techniques daily just to get through life. By understanding how the mind works, we can start utilising the techniques to make changes in our minds.

Visualisation

We have already touched on the aspects of talking the correct talk and using mantras, which I use every day when I am falling asleep or when opening my eyes in the morning. I have also touched upon writing down your goals and putting them in a prominent place so they can be seen regularly and just before you fall asleep. Jim Carrey famously wrote himself a post-dated cheque for $10 million for acting services. He kept that cheque in his wallet and within three years, using hard work and various techniques of visualisation, he achieved his goal.

For any real big challenge in life, the above can make a huge difference, but we need to bring out the big guns here to maximise the outcome. The main technique that I use for that is visualisation and/or imagination.

I mention visualisation AND/OR imagination, because for some of us it's hard to visualise anything. If I ask most people to visualise themselves driving the car of their dreams, they are able to close their eyes and bring to mind a perfect image of themselves driving that car, maybe have the hood down, but they will have clear images. Others do not have that ability to visualise, and I am one of them. If you ask me to close my eyes and visualise something, all I will see is black. So, if you, like me, are unable to bring up an image in your mind, turn to imagination. For the above scenario, I would have a constant internal verbal dialogue going on in my head talking myself through exactly what it would be like to drive that car, the feelings I would be experiencing, and the emotions I would be going through. Visualisation is not something we are all gifted with so sometimes we have to use other senses.

When I was preparing for the English Channel swim, I was fortunate to have a 25-minute train ride to work and back every day. I was also lucky enough to get a seat! As soon as I got on the train, I sat down, closed my eyes and started slowing my breathing down by taking deeper and more controlled breaths. At the same time, I started visualising my swim. From preparing to get on the boat and the trip to the start, to togging up, applying sun-cream, going through the paperwork, diving in and then starting my swim, experiencing every scenario that my mind could conceive of until I finally walked up to the finishing line. I then got off the train and started my day. I did this on nearly every train journey. In my visualisations, the start and finish were ALWAYS the same, the content in between varied wildly with as many ridiculous scenarios as I could dream up. When I first started doing this, I often just carried on through the levels into my sleep levels and fell asleep and even occasionally ended up at the wrong station - only to have to call my wife to come and fetch me!

The more I did it, the more I was able to hone it down to a fine art - where I would jump on the train, go through my visualisation (spending 25 minutes visualising and imagining the whole scenario) and then open my eyes as we pulled in to my station, collect my bag and walk out of the train at the correct place.

I was approached by fellow travellers and asked how the heck I could just close my eyes and "sleep" - and then wake up at exactly the right moment as the train was pulling into the station! They were all too scared to do it as they feared falling into slumber land and missing their stop. What they did not realise was that I was not actually sleeping but playing through a movie about my swim in my mind. I was going through all the pitfalls I could dream of and playing out exactly how I would deal with them.

Being able to just switch off for 25 minutes is also related to our brain cycles. Often you will hear people talk of having the ability to catnap. This is the ability to drift off to sleep and slow our brain rhythms down but then wake up before we disappear into Theta levels. For me, this is about 20-25 minutes. At that point I can wake up feeling refreshed and revitalised. It infuriates the Slimhippo that I have this ability! The alternative is that we will carry on into deep sleep, often for about an hour or two. For example, if you are one of the lucky ones who has the time for an afternoon siesta, you go to sleep and set an alarm for an hour or two later. What often happens is that the alarm will wake you when you are at your slowest level of low Theta or Delta. This is the worst time to be woken, as you will wake feeling lethargic and more often than not, more drowsy (and often more grumpy) than you were before you went off for your siesta. This is because you have woken up from a deep sleep rather than from a very light sleep.

Visualisation is by far one of the most powerful ways to input a new belief into your mind. Nowadays, it is used in nearly every aspect of life and it can either be done sitting calmly and visualising the outcome or can be a lot more physical in nature.

If you have ever watched racing drivers, Red Bull air racers, rally drivers or cyclists, they can often be seen before an event with their eyes closed enacting out the entire course that they are going to drive or race. They are visualising every turn, bump, corner, and junction - and more importantly, they are visualising what they are doing at all of these. What gear will I be in? What are the revs of the engine? The gradient I am climbing? What does the engine sound like? And so on and so on. The more information they can visualise or imagine in order to make that visual training as REAL as possible, the better. They do this as often as they can, so by the time they come to race, they have done that race in their head a hundred, maybe a thousand times. By the time I actually swam the Channel, I had swum it about a thousand times in my head.

So how exactly could you employ this strategy for something like swimming the Channel? We can all agree that is it not the most scintillating sport in the world. This is where imagination and visualisation can work extremely well together. Now imagination can be difficult for many adults. It is one of the abilities that has kind of deserted us along the way, having been overtaken by routine, regimes and protocol, leading to a loss of spontaneity and improvisation. A saying that comes to mind here is "you can lead a human to knowledge, but you cannot make them think!" It also makes me laugh just thinking about how someone might ACTIVELY visualise a Channel swim on something like a train journey. Watching someone flailing their arms about, writhing on the floor with their eyes closed taking deep gasping breaths might raise a few eyebrows from some of your fellow passengers. Mind you, in London, it is also possible no one would even notice!

Fortunately, our mind is our own and we are hopefully in control of it. If, like me, you have the luxury of sitting on a train for 25 minutes into work and 25 minutes back home, then this is an ideal time for visualisation and imagination. In my head I have mentally built a cinema, like no other cinema on the planet. It has EVERYTHING I need and desire in a cinema. It is my mind, I built it. When I used to travel anywhere by train, I would spend a few minutes unwrapping myself from the busy bustling world I exist in and enter into my world, my office, my cinema. For every challenge that I had I would spend time watching a movie in my head – well, I say watch, but as I am not a very visual person, my imagination, and internal verbal dialogue worked for me. The movies I had created were of my various dreamed up challenges. For instance, a trip across the English Channel holds many obstacles, all there to challenge you and to test your mettle. I watched myself swimming across the Channel many, many times. Each time, the results were exactly the same - I started and I finished, but every other aspect changed every time I swam it.

My internal verbal dialogue also spills over into when I am physically doing something like this. I am often asked, "What do you think about for 12 hours – whilst you are swimming?" Some recite poetry, sing songs, and imagine their favourite cars/calendars/motorbikes. For me, I am talking myself through, making sure that I am gliding through the water as efficiently as I possibly can. Is my breathing good, is my arm entry good, is my glide good, is my stretch at its best, is my body position working properly? During the tougher moments of a challenge, I have actually verbally sworn at myself with so much gusto that the thoughts have become full blown – *spoken* - word, and the next thing I know, I have taken in a HUGE gulp of sea water, the resulting choking immediately stopping me in my tracks! All these tasks I mentally talk myself through the whole time. Yes, it is a long time to be swimming but if you keep your mind active and occupied, there is very little time for it to start letting those negative thoughts in. The hardest challenge is to keep those thoughts at bay.

During my preparation, in my head, I experienced jellyfish, freezing temperatures, irritating crew, and bad pilots (not that there are any, but I had to prepare). I swam at night, during the day, through rain, hail, freezing nights, awesome sunsets, grey clouds. I finished the swim on a beach, on the rocks, near the harbours. I crossed and encountered ferries, speed boats, tankers (the one time I even had to swim underneath a tanker to avoid being run over!). There were times that it was serenely calm, and others when it was blowing a gale and I lost the pilot boat due to the swell. I was bitten by seals, experienced back ache, shoulder ache, groin ache, my legs seized up, my shoulders seized, I tore muscles - you name it, I visualised it and emotionally I wrecked myself. I experienced EVERY CONCEIVABLE ADVERSITY in the intimacy of my personal mind cinema. With each adverse situation, I devised a way that I was going to deal with it, how I was going to react and how I was going to keep going no matter what. With the help of my imagination and mantras, all these obstacles were encountered again and again, and all of them were overcome.

During your swim, barring any physical mishaps like serious injury, your mind will be the first thing to go and your body will then follow suit. Spending time calmly in my mind experiencing the worst and best of the challenge is a powerful form of mental preparation for me, for any event. My mind, and in response my body, are more able to deal with the problems that arise. If what I believe is true, that your mind controls your entire being, preparing for the best and the worst that a challenge can throw at you is vital and, like learning to do anything, the more you do it the more proficient you become, and the more your mind becomes ready.

I often find that people with very vivid imaginations or a great ability to visualise things (yes, you guessed it – children) are much better at setting up a new programme in their mind than those with less ability to imagine. Be creative - what happens in your mind is yours and yours alone, nobody but you will have access to it so you can literally go wild with the most outlandish scenarios you can create. It is also always good to envisage how the body will react and the feelings and emotions that will go with what you are imagining. Any way that you can get your mind and body to mimic the idea of what you will experience is a good thing.

One problem with the mind when trying to imagine or visualise things, is that most people get into the trap that while they are making time to do it, they spend more time worrying about whether they are in the right brain state or not. Thus, the overall experience and benefit of the process is lost, as worry and anxiety predominate in the Beta level and when you are trying to relax while worrying, it is counterproductive. To get around this you HAVE TO be confident that you will cycle up and down through all the levels. Especially at night when preparing for sleep, you WILL go from Beta to Alpha and then into Theta. Be sure that you will spend time in the Alpha level so go ahead with your visualisation/imagination and go wild. Chances are you will fall asleep but that is not a problem as, while you are falling asleep, you'll go down through your levels.

Chapter 9: Pain and Injury management

I am guessing that the first thing that entered your mind when you read the above heading for the next chapter is, PAINKILLERS! It is readily assumed that ultra-distance athletes, whether swimming, running, or cycling, will resort to all kinds of painkillers such as ibuprofen and paracetamol to keep their pain and their injuries managed. Just four weeks before my English Channel swim I was at the doctors with an injured shoulder, and the doctor's advice was painkillers and more importantly REST. With only four weeks before, what for me was the biggest physical challenge of my life, the latter was definitely off the cards and I told the doctor that I would not be doing any resting. Painkillers were offered, and I did take a few, but I just kept swimming regardless.

Preparation for these events is obviously essential, and the more aspects I can use to maximise that preparation, using not only my physical attributes and training but my mental and emotional preparation, is just as important. I have found though that in the eleven years that I have been doing these events, everyone is very motivated by the physical side of the training. I have seen many cases of "burnout", and more worryingly, injury, before the main event even starts. My opinion on this is that I would rather have undertrained physically and be certain that I am in a good physical condition when I arrive at the start, rather than having done thousands of kilometres in the lead up, only to damage my body before I even begin.

So how did I get over this injury and continue to swim injury free for the next 4 weeks and during my 21-mile journey across the English Channel? I turned to a technique that utilises my mind which is also another great way to keep your mind busy.

A very useful implementation of visualisation and imagination is when you are actually doing your challenge, or you are getting through a training event. Any ultra-distance event can be boring, and they do not come as boring and mundane as swimming for 10 – 20 hours. With very little external stimuli to occupy your mind, you must come up with other ways to keep your mind focused and positive thoughts at the fore, and keep the negative and destructive thoughts at bay. Not only can our mind be a very powerful tool to prepare for such events, it can be very useful to maintain your body at its optimum throughout the event. It goes without saying that a trip across the Channel may involve somewhere near 250000 strokes. Take into account all the training, and there are often many millions of strokes in the lead up to this. With that sort of effort, there is bound to be wear and tear on the body, especially the shoulders, hips and groin area.

I believe that monitoring and repairing my body while I swim is a key part to my successful swims and the fact that I regularly do swims without any form of pain relief. Generally, my recovery from all my swims is within the ten-hour region before I can do it all again. Yes, this does sound ludicrous. How the heck can you monitor and repair your body while you are swimming, when it is usually in the Delta region of our brain waves that our body will repair and rejuvenate itself? No, I am not fast asleep while I am swimming - although some might argue otherwise (I often swim with my eyes closed).

This is where things get a bit weird. Let me invite you back to the "office" that I mentioned earlier. Not only is there a state-of-the-art cinema, I have my own personal army of surgeons, physiotherapists, doctors, chiropractors and masseuses. I call them my minions. I also have a state-of-the-art pharmacy and operating theatre. They are on call all the time and with their advanced facilities, their funky minion mobiles – to get to the areas needed, the best ointments and pills that the wildest imagination could dream of. They can fix my body and repair my muscles when I am on the move. So you may ask what I do with my mind when I am swimming. Well, whenever I have twinges or pains starting to attack my body, I despatch a team to the area to go and fix the problem before it becomes an issue. Not only can I have a massage whilst I am swimming, I can replace individual muscle fibres and cartilage at any time that I want to.

Again, using the power of visualisation, or in my case – mental dialogue, I can carry out emergency procedures while I am swimming. It is your mind - you can decide exactly how you are going to fix any issues that start to appear. Having a warped sense of humour and a penchant for the utter ridiculous definitely helps too! Recently on my lengthier lake swims, where I have a boat beside me, I have taken to swimming with my eyes closed most of the time. This gives me the ability to disappear into my cinema or my utopia – again, created in my own mind. It gives me the ability to focus inwardly by blocking out the stimuli of sight. I will swim like this for ages, occasionally opening my eyes when I breathe to make sure that I am still with the boat. It is not always a good plan when swimming in oceans as one of the things that you need to be wary about in the oceans is jellyfish swarms. Swimming into them is not the nicest thing to do and although I have the ability to deal with them in my head, the pain is still pretty alarming when you do. The key is, the more I can disappear inwardly, then the more comfortable I am with my swims. I have often heard marathon swimming being described as "My happy place" by many athletes – this is my version.

Again, this must come with a belief that it will work. On that basis I would rather have the belief that the possibility is there, that it does work. I really cannot say one way or another if it does or how, but I have 10 – 20 hours to kill so I might as well utilise it productively.

From what you have learnt in this, and the last chapter, the more cynical reader may very well say that I am not in the right brain level for all of this to be effective. I would disagree entirely. Another form of slowing our brains down is to use the endorphins created from exercise to transport yourself into a more meditative state. One of the swims that I have taken part in is the Sri Chinmoy Lake Zurich marathon swim. His entire foundation is based on transcending or moving past your current abilities through endurance events. Many ultra-distance athletes can attest that their endurance can take them out of our normal consciousness into a different state of mind beyond the usual thoughts and emotions. For many, these events can very often be a form of meditation. In this way, by using your 'happy place' you can achieve a heightened level, which will allow you to focus and get you through the tough stuff. I urge you to figure out your 'happy place' and visit it as often as you can during your preparation.

Chapter 10 – Nutrition

On this I have my own very personal plan, it is by no means scientific and by no means useful to anyone else out there, as we all differ in what we can use without side effects and also what we like to use. A common side effect that I have come across is vomiting. Regularly, people throw up during their swims and this can be down to various things such as bloating, salt ingestion whilst breathing, seasickness, or electrolyte imbalance. Another common affliction is dizziness, and while this may be related to nutrition, there can be other causes as well. Our bodies are pretty complex, with everything in careful balance, so there are many things that may need tweaking to reduce any unwanted reactions.

One thing I learnt in my last swim on Loch Lomond, is that all feeding plans are fallible. I had my plan all worked out. Thanks to the nagging of the Slimhippo, I even had it all printed out, all my feeds mixed at different strengths, solid food at the ready. I had some hot water for me if I got cold and needed warm food. I had food for my support crew, so we were all good, I thought. But with water temperatures hovering between 13 and 14°C, my usual tricks of trying to warm myself up were all futile. Then, after 3 hours, the swim started to go downhill rapidly, as I was approaching hypothermia and I began to hyperventilate. Things had to change and FAST. My feeding plan had to be ditched and a new one implemented. Thanks to my amazing support team, who now had to do some quick thinking and come up with a new plan - the feeds all now had to be hot or warmed up. We also had to switch from hourly feeds to half hourly feeds so that my condition could be monitored more regularly. Sadly for the support crew, I used nearly all the hot water on board for me, and they had little to feed themselves and keep themselves warm on an 11.5 hour overnight swim down a Scottish loch. Luckily the rain held off for most the swim, so they were only cold, not wet and cold for the entire swim. I always knew that immersing a body that is usually around 37°C into water that is less than half that would always result in a sapping of energy and body heat. I have swum in much colder water than that but only for about thirty minutes and my six-hour qualifier was done in 15.8°C with the sun on my back the whole time. Without better acclimation, my feeding plan became crucial, and fortunately the warm feeds (amongst other things) got me through.

In this chapter I will give you a brief overview of what I have done nutrition wise, but then I will have to ask for assistance from another marathon swimmer friend and Doctor who is far more qualified in this sphere than I will ever be. He has kindly put forward an article on this very contentious issue.

First let us look at one way – the way I have done it and continue to do it.

When I started in this game, I had NO idea about nutrition and still to this day have very little scientific knowledge. As mentioned, I found what worked for me and use that regime to this day. The choice of the day was Maxim™, which is a maltodextrin based fuel that I mixed to about four times the recommended strength; I also had a bottle of normal strength. My feeding plan was based on what I was taught at the time and it hasn't really changed much. Again, the following is just an outline of what can be used, but by no means may be a system that will work for you.

My regime was based on the fact that I was very confident that I can go for about 2 hours without any food.

Before an event - drink about 250ml of my extra strength juice JUST before starting (I mention this because, if I want to get away from the bloating, the energy drink I take on has to be utilised quickly, so literally JUST before the start).

2 hours – 250ml normal strength juice with some fruit

3 hours – 250ml normal strength juice with a chocolate or jelly babies

4 hours – 250ml normal strength juice with a few sips of half Coke, half water**

5 hours – 250ml of extra strength with some solid food (fruit or biscuits) plus electrolyte mix

6 hours – 250ml of normal strength followed by a few sips of Listerine mix*

7 hours – 250ml of normal strength with some solid food

8 hours- 250ml of normal strength with a few sips of lukewarm tea with honey

9 hours – 250ml of normal strength with some fruit or biscuits or jelly babies, electrolyte mix

10 hours – 250ml of extra strength with some solid food

11 hours – Half Coke, half water followed by a few sips of Listerine mix

12 hours - 250ml of normal strength

- * Listerine™ is a very powerful mouthwash and is used to just freshen up your mouth a bit. As it is very strong and your mouth may be suffering from a bit of swelling or worse, due to the salt, I mix it to about a 10 % mixture, so it does not hurt my already vulnerable mouth.
- ** Half Coke half water; I do this as I like Coke but at full strength it is too gassy for me.

For solid foods, I use a lot of fruit - mangos, melons, citrus and chopped up apples. For biscuits I use chocolate coated biscuits.

As you can see, not very scientific at all, and the basis of having the extra strength is that if I at least pump myself full of energy, then the energy side of things is taken care of. All that is required is to keep going.

Nowadays there is a huge amount of research that has gone into sports nutrition from the nutrition to the recovery, to the maintenance of electrolytes whilst undergoing an event and after the event. All of which are vitally important to keep in balance. Maxim™ for me, has been replaced by CNP™ which is very similar to Maxim™ but results in less bloating and is much easier on the stomach.

This is where I need to ask for assistance on a more modern day approach and Dr Nicholas Murch, an extremely accomplished marathon swimmer, who is far more accomplished than I in both nutrition and swimming, has kindly written an article and let me use it in this book.

Nutrition in Channel swimming: Bonkers behaviour?

There is little more in endurance sport that divides opinion as much as the subject of nutrition. So I thought I would put my feelings down to enable others to benefit from what I have learned in my open water swimming and medical career to date. I swam the English Channel and Lake Geneva in 2016 and have worked as medical support in the High Dependency Unit at the end of the London Marathon on at least two occasions. Some of this may be controversial or against accepted thought, but then I'm all about a debate and there is no 'one size fits all' plan.

Basically, the take home message is that there is no right answer, so you don't need to read on. If you do, I'll use some science to make the point.

Most people use a carbohydrate gel or solution to feed whilst marathon swimming. These are usually composed of small molecules that provide rapid release energy but can cause the stomach to distend (causing nausea) and may have, in my opinion, laxative effects. Many distance athletes get "runners' trots" (think a certain female marathon runner) and this may be due to excessive pure water consumption, the laxative effect of feeding agents and diversion of blood away from the bowels to the muscles. It is not dirty water that (usually) causes swimmers to develop gastrointestinal upset.

Some maths:

The body's main stores for aerobic exercise are approximately, for an 80 kilogram (kg) man:

(Note carbohydrate and protein both store 4 calories/gram and fat 9 calories/gram)

Glycogen (carbohydrate) in liver: 120 grams = 480 calories

Glycogen in muscles: 350 grams = 1400 calories

Fat stored throughout body: 16kg (20 percent body weight) fat: 144,000 calories

Protein can make up to 5 percent of energy requirements but is not ideal to break down when exercising, so we will ignore it for now.

Therefore, there are only 1880 calories worth of carbohydrate stored in the body of an 80kg man.

In extreme prolonged sport it is possible to use 700 to 800 calories per hour, but the maximum carbohydrate replacement intake is suggested at approx.:

Maximum <1 gram/kg/hr – 60 to 90 grams per hour so 240 to 360 calories per hour – let's say 320 calories for an 80kg male.

Many people feed hourly or half hourly in long distance swimming. There is clearly a mismatch in intake versus exhausted calories (cals) available in carbohydrate form. For example:

Hour 1: 1880 cals to start, 800 cals exhausted, 320 cals taken in = 1400 calories left

Hour 2: 1400 cals to start, 800 cals exhausted, 320 cals taken in = 920 calories left

Hour 3: 920 cals to start, 800 cals exhausted, 320 cals taken in = 440 calories left

Hour 4: 440 cals to start, 800 cals exhausted – this means a 360 calorie deficit with max intake 320 calories... and the body must switch to an alternative fuel source.

This is where **fat metabolism** comes in to play. The body must break down fat stores to create energy, which may promote the development of molecules called ketones which can make the blood slightly acidic in some individuals. This can be uncomfortable if unanticipated and leads to the stage of an endurance event where one 'hits the wall' or 'bonks'. This occurs very early in a Channel crossing, and so the body needs to be able to cope in that environment.

Simple carbohydrate ingestion (e.g. CNP™/ Maxim™ etc.) may cause spikes in blood sugar levels and a reflex release of insulin, which blocks the body from breaking down fat, so those jelly babies or energy drinks may actually be hampering physical performance in the long term. Ways to minimise the 'glycaemic rollercoaster' may be to feed regularly on small amounts or to have a more sustained released carbohydrate mixture (e.g. UCAN™).

I'm a big believer than we should train as we mean to fight – and so I spent several weeks on a low carbohydrate, high protein, high fat diet while preparing for my English Channel crossing (21 miles, 11 hours) and Lake Geneva traverse (69km, 32 hours). I would also train for up to 7 hours with just a coffee beforehand and the odd sugary treat every hour – clearly relying on my 'bioprene' to provide the majority of my energy whilst swimming.

Whilst on the subject of coffee, many people are either for or against **caffeine** during exercise. I, for one, have at least five coffees a day so if I didn't have a caffeinated drink during a long swim, I would likely get withdrawal symptoms. If naïve to caffeine, then I would strongly advise against taking it during exercise.

One nutrient we cannot do without is **water** – the body needs 25 to 30 mls/kg/day maintenance hydration (i.e. when not exercising) which equates to 2 to 2.4 litres for the 80kg athlete plus insensible losses (sweating, heat, water lost on extra deep breathing etc.). Hydration is key for prime athletic performance. East African marathon runners traditionally used tea as their means of hydration and ran at approximately 2 to 3 percent dehydration as optimal offset of performance versus weight. Anything more than 5 percent dehydration causes a massive drop off in performance. Swimmers are less worried about weight due to relative buoyancy so must stay hydrated to maintain performance. Excessive pre-hydration however, may predispose to fluid overload such as swimming induced pulmonary oedema.

Pure water may cause problems too though, as salt (sodium) is also lost in sweat and replacement with pure water may cause a dilution of the blood which can cause problems with both physical performance and health. I personally do not subscribe to the argument that being in saltwater will replace salt lost in sweat so I take an **electrolyte** supplement containing sodium, potassium, chloride and magnesium (amongst others). There are some basic electrolytes in some of the branded carbohydrate drinks so read the label!

The main reason for a periodic feed is, in my mind, two-fold. One is for a psychological lift to have some human contact, and to look forward to that placebo effect Jelly baby. One truly swims to the next feed in times of hardship. The other is for the crew to assess how you are performing and whether you are hypothermic, hallucinating etc. We have a certain individual on Swimmers beach in Dover that swam the Channel on a full English breakfast and many others just on water alone.

The take home message is to train as you mean to fight – train on empty and consider running ketogenic at times (not if you are diabetic – this can be dangerous). Keep feeding regimes, and hence your metabolism, versatile and do what works for you – even if it is psychological.

Thank you Dr Murch!

For a lot of people, they come into this game with little or no experience on how to feed. There may be a lot of thoughts thrown about at local training on what to do. In this case it is best to DO AS YOU ARE TOLD. If you are fortunate to train with other people aspiring to the same goal, where there are a group of people looking after you, just do what they tell you and stick to it – unless of course it does not really agree with you. IF there is some disagreement with your system, the time to alter and play around with your feeding regime and try to find out what works for you, is in the training - not a week before your event. Sudden changes can wreak havoc out in open water. It may also be necessary to change your regime mid-challenge, so be aware of this.

One aspect to take into account when you are on an ocean challenge such as the Channel is the time that it takes to feed. This becomes very important when you are in the middle of the Channel with the tides running at their quickest. Remember the one-armed breaststroke mentioned earlier in the drills - this can come in useful when feeding. At the professional end of this game, swimmers will often roll onto their back and take one or two backstrokes whilst gulping down their food and then roll back on to their front to continue. The aim is to spend as little time as possible immobile.

Should the swim require an elaborate feeding plan, ALL preparation should be done the night before. Preparing on the day just adds further stress to an already emotionally charged day. Mix all your feeds ahead of time, make sure you have the tools and gadgets needed to accomplish your feeding. Checklists are a good thing; even though I virtually never bother with such things, this is **one time** that I do - and even then, I have been found wanting. Another good piece of advice is to make sure that you change the time on your various gadgets when you are travelling, as arriving at an event late because your alarm went off late is not a good way to start!

When it comes to travelling internationally, be sure to pack your feeds in your hand luggage rather than in checked in baggage. If you've arrived at the start of an event sans baggage, you won't be left scrambling around to find what you need.

Another thing to think of is that in nearly all the bigger swims, you are not allowed to touch the boat at all, so how are you going to feed? This can be very boat dependant. If your support is on a kayak, they may not need anything to get the feed or food down to the swimmer but if they are on more of an ocean crossing with a motorised boat, then they may need some way of handing food to the swimmer even though they are far away from you. The best thing to do here is to use the KISS principle – Keep It Simple Stupid! The more elaborate the contraption, the more possibilities for it to go wrong. Contraptions that I have seen used range from the sublime to the ridiculous, but the simpler the better. As you want to keep your feeds as short as possible, it is not a good idea to give the swimmer multiple things to deal with when they feed as this will just take up too much time. The best is one bottle and maybe some solids.

For all my bottles, I now use a retractable dog lead that my support crew will attach to the bottle. The bottle is left sealed but easy to open and is dropped into the water. If I need more slack, I can just pull out the retractable lead. I then leave the bottle in the water for my support team to retrieve. For my solid foods, I generally have them all prepared and cut up before hand, and by using a retractable

166

pole with a piece of Tupperware attached, it can be held out for me to take what I want. Another useful tip is to tether the retractable pole and the retractable lead to the boat so, if they are dropped for any reason, they can be retrieved.

Chapter 11: The journey continues

Now that you are well under way into your adventures, the next thing that you need to worry about is momentum. Whether your goal lasts a few months or even some years, however you go about it, make the best use of your time and your resources. There is a heck of a lot of information out there nowadays about how people did this or that and how they got to their goals. If there is one thing I have learnt time and time again, information is very useful but your plan has to revolve around you, your circumstances and what you can and cannot do. Take the information and with the use of a coach – if you use one, adapt that information to your needs.

Having made the decision to take on a challenge like this and while talking about it in the correct way to yourself and to others (whether they believe you or not), nothing makes it more real in your mind than having to dig into your bank balance to pay for the deposit for the boat. This can be a pretty big chunk of money and for me, doing this was the single most prominent moment where I moved from "I am going to swim the Channel" to "Oh MY God, what the hell am I doing!!" This suddenly became *very real* in my head.

My slot was booked and I had a date in my head. Bear in mind that this date was by no means set in stone. I was on the beach at Dover 5 weeks before my allocated time slot when Alison came down to the beach looking for me. I was due to be in the water for four hours. She mentioned that, if I wanted to, a slot had become available the following day, starting at about 7am. Would I like to take it?

My mind went into overdrive. Could I get my crew down here, bearing in mind that I would probably have to find some alternative crew at such short notice? I did not have all that I needed with me, so it would have meant a trip back to Surrey to pick up the rest of my stuff, then come straight back down. My parents would not be able to share my experience with me. But then I could at least have a great break with them when they arrived without the thought of a Channel swim hanging over me. OH SO MANY thoughts were rushing through my head. The biggest one being – AM I ready for this challenge? I would have to borrow the small shortfall to fully pay for this adventure! So I said to Alison that I would go and swim for two hours and would let her know after that if I was going to take up the offer or not. She was fine with that. After mulling all this over in my head, I declined the offer in favour of sticking to my slot. Now I was swamped with thoughts about whether I was doing the right thing? Would I live to regret that decision? Only time would tell. I knew full well that with my slot being so late in the season, if it was by some chance blown out then I would not get to swim that year, and it would all have to be postponed to another year. I was taking a big risk by not taking this opportunity, but I desperately wanted to share this experience with my parents.

What keeps up your drive or momentum is very different for each person. For me, it was my health that was my driving force, amongst other things, but for many it is a very personal goal, often one that they have had for a long time. An enormous amount of money is raised for charity by Channel swimmers as well, and many use this as motivation. Charity work can be the start of bigger things, but involves the people around you, you get to meet some amazing people, and do some good at the same time. However, it can also add a fair amount of 'admin' to an already busy life. It does get you to move out of your comfort zone in a different direction though, and to be the ambassador for a certain cause is fulfilling. While you are already on an amazing journey that will move you into circles you never dreamed of, charity drives will broaden that circle even more.

As I have mentioned before, invest this time wisely. Surround yourself with the right people, and consider all forms of training such as Masters classes, pool sets, Yoga, Pilates, or weights and circuit training, to give you a broader range of fitness and a change up from those sets in the pool.

Remember that technique is a major contributor to what your final time will be in the challenge. The difference between someone who swims at 5km an hour and someone who swims at 3km an hour can be a difference of between four and eight hours of swimming, so know your expectations and train or prepare accordingly. If you are happy as a slower swimmer, then prepare for a longer swim. If you do not want to prepare for a longer swim, then invest time and money in professional technique training. If you are someone who has swum for years, be prepared for the time it will take to change your technique. In any technique training, it always seems like you go backwards before you go forwards. This is getting your body and muscles out of bad habits and into good habits, and like most habits, you must be prepared to put this time in. Putting in loads of time in the water is not going to make you any quicker unless you are willing to work on a technique that will make you quicker. I very often see people just ploughing up and down, up and down and never really getting any better or faster.

A regular hole that I fell into was to read and learn about others taking on the same challenge and then become very despondent about the fact that they were doing up to four times as much distance that I was. This really played on my mind and really affected my training to the point where I would finish a session then go and log on and read that someone had done a heck of a lot more than me and beat myself up. This changed when I decided to stop reading what others were doing and finally got to train with some people that were chasing the same goal. What I noticed made me feel a lot better. Whilst they were doing a LOT more than I was able to do, my (shorter) training sessions were done at a very high intensity to the point where I was absolutely exhausted, whilst those that had done more training, albeit at a much slower pace, were far less exhausted. This comes back to the question I have posed earlier in this book: what is better, high intensity or high mileage? Again, the answer will be very specific to you and your circumstances.

Personally, I like to do the high intensity rather than the high mileage.

The open water swimming community is very inclusive, supportive and a great place to find a swimming partner and form lifelong friendships. When I arrived at Dover on the first weekend of season, I knew no one, but over time I trained with others who were all on the same path - some fast, some slow, the majority of us of the more rotund build, whilst others were very slim. The group was immensely diverse. Over a few swims I found someone who was to become my training partner, my support crew and a lifelong friend. Greg Wood, who was also training to swim the Channel that year, lived in Kent; he was a bit younger than me, a LOT slimmer than I was, but we swam at very similar speeds. Greg was the wise guy who took mixing things up to a whole new level when he decided that, after three hours of swimming in the harbour, it would be a good idea to sprint a length of the harbour. Yes, a 1200m sprint is a pretty mad way to mix things up, but he was also instrumental in getting me moving. Whenever we used to reach one side of the harbour, we would tread water and chat for a while, and it was generally Greg who got me moving again. Due to him being a lot slimmer than me, he could not wallow as well as a hippo can, so his objective was to keep moving.

All in all, I trained with a very diverse and very talented group of people, all with the same objective in mind. As the season progresses, swimmers start to go across the Channel in about late June/early July, so as the season wears on, swimmers take on their challenge either successfully or unsuccessfully. This is often the hardest part of the season - seeing people that have put so much effort into their goal be unsuccessful. Generally, they appear at the beach again for a few weeks and then get back to their lives. As my swim was at the end of the season, of the ninety odd swimmers that had been there at the beginning, there were only a handful left on the beach at the weekends towards the end of September. This brought on a whole set of new emotions, as the buzz on the beach began to die down. You follow the swimmers and then they are gone. You get to the point where you have watched so many people take on their swims that you really start missing the camaraderie on the beach. I was now cursing myself that I did not take the opportunity to take my swim earlier in the season, when Alison had offered it to me. Again, this is a double edged sword as you start the season with loads of people with big dreams and high hopes - by the end of the season they are all gone so you are left doing your 6 – 8 hour swims entirely on your own, which is an amazing time to get in the boredom training.

All too soon, five months after my very first dip in the salty murky waters of Dover harbour and my very first swim in the ocean, it was time for me to take on the challenge of a lifetime.

Chapter 12: Cold water acclimation

In any challenge there will be obstacles along the way and that is no different when it comes to open water swimming, depending where and when your challenge will take place. One thing that is very apparent in any water-based sport is the climate that you will have to deal with. With swimming, the main issue that you might get to experience, unless you live, and plan to permanently train and compete in the tropics, is the temperature - not only of the water, but also the outside air. For most of the events globally, there WILL be a need to get into water that you will not find in any leisure centre pool. Usually, in Britain, they will be maintained at a very toasty 26-30°C. A standard marathon swim is generally classed as 10km (this is what they do in the Olympics). For most endurance swims out there, that is a mere training swim. For a vast majority of the European swims, the water temperature will be more like 17°C (62° Fahrenheit). And, if you are into the fast-growing ice swimming arm of this sport, that temperature probably drops another twelve degrees. Yes, in ice swimming you are not aiming on spending 6 hours in there, but the challenge is brutal and in a completely different league.

With the plethora of swims that are popping up around the globe classed in the endurance category, there are now many ocean, lake or river based swims that are over three times the length of what is considered a marathon swim. If a world class time for 10km marathon swim is around the two-hour mark, you can see that the time spent in the water is going to be 6 -7 hours. The record for the English Channel is 6 hours and 55 minutes. So for the vast majority, we will most likely be in the water for double if not triple that time. So cold water acclimation is a key ingredient for any endurance swim.

So, how do you go about this? There are many schools of thought out there - some verging on the insane to the more sedate approaches.

Although I haven't tried or tested them, ice baths, cold showers and extreme cold immersion have been advocated - but then I do live in Britain where we can have a fairly brisk winter. That, combined with the fact that I have a fifteen minute walk to a train station and a five to ten minute wait for a train at least twice a day, my chosen theory was that I would not use a jersey/sweater/ jacket during the winter preceding a cold water swim. I would walk to the station in temperatures hovering just above freezing in jeans and t-shirt and possibly a Gilet (sleeveless jacket) to protect my core. I would wait around in the cold then jump onto a train and do the same on the other side and repeat on the return journey home. This served two purposes: getting my body used to the cold and also getting used to hot flushes. Another unexpected reaction to me wondering around in just jeans and t-shirts was the amount people that I met whilst carrying out this acclimatisation. Many a concerned citizen would come up to me on the platform and ask me if I was okay? Heck, I was going to swim the English Channel so I will leave you to make up your mind on that! There were no cold showers and no ice baths, just getting out into the cold as much as possible. During the winter I still did my winter training in the warmth of the leisure pool, although I did find swimming the longer sets in 27°C heated pools very draining. There were times on a heavy set that I honestly felt that I was going to self-combust, so on an average day I would go from walking round in freezing temperatures to burning up in the pool - all good for acclimatisation. The outcome of this was that I was far more comfortable in water that was about 14 -16°C. Having said that, getting into water at these temperatures still takes my breath away and I have to carry out some fairly rigorous controlled breathing to get over the initial shock. As the saying goes, it is great once you are in.

As the season progressed through the summer and the ambient temperatures rose, I ventured out into the lakes when they opened and then into the ocean. At the start of the season it is generally about 10 – 12°C in the lakes and rivers and slightly warmer (13 – 15°C) in the oceans. When venturing into these temperatures for the first time, I took very short dips of about 20 – 30 minutes, possibly two or three times a day, and then just increased the time in the water at those temperatures. Bear in mind there is a direct correlation at first that the colder the water is, the shorter the time you can swim comfortably. A similar opposite effect is seen when training in warm pools – it gets harder to do big distances.

There are the other more extreme approaches and one of them is to swim all year round without a wetsuit. Nowadays you do not look like a complete nutcase. With the explosion of ice and wild swimming that is happening around the globe, you are usually not very far from a group of mad men and women who embrace the elements and just love throwing themselves into almost, or in some cases, completely frozen lakes to get their kicks and also to acclimatise to the cold. I have to mention here that this comes with a warning. NEVER DO THIS ALONE and NEVER IMMERSE YOURSELF FOR TOO LONG. One season, this whole ice swimming started to intrigue me, so I decided as an experiment, I would give it a try purely to see if I could find my limits and to see what my physiological responses were. So with zero experience, I found myself on the edge of the Jubilee River in the midst of winter, with a group that swim all year round in the rivers, some with wetsuits and some sans wetsuit. The first time I went into water that was hovering 2 -3°C above freezing, I was in for about fifteen minutes and had reached the point where although being a bit chilly, I was extremely comfortable and FELT as if I could have gone on much further. I was subsequently told that I was nearing the point of hypothermia! Take this approach very cautiously and prepare to have your kit immediately available so that you can warm up in a controlled way post swim. Most importantly, keep it short at first.

Leading heart surgeons around the world who have swum oceans warn against this absurd approach, but it does not stop a hardcore group of cold-water swimmers from venturing out into freezing lakes and waterways. At temperatures just above freezing, the euphoria achieved once you have done a cold-water swim and managed to successfully warm up afterwards is amazing. Your body feels incredible - even though it may look like you have spent the day on a hot sunny beach in the Bahamas without sunscreen! The key to post cold water swim recovery is to warm yourself up slowly. Here is a basic physiological description that I was given as to what happens:

(This is not scientific and is just what I have learnt and been told)

When entering the cold water initially, the first reaction you will have to fight against is the cold-water shock response. Mind you, I get that response even in temperatures nearing 20°C!

This will generally only last for about 1 – 4 minutes and it can, if not controlled, have a direct effect on your breathing, as there will normally be a gasp reflex in response to the rapid skin cooling. This gasp can be detrimental, especially if you dive or jump into the cold water. The gasping can result in accidental water inhalation with serious effects. There are various ways in which people approach their entry into extremely cold water. Below lists a few of those chosen ways:

1. Walk into the water up to your waist and stand in the water for a minute, splashing your upper body, torso and shoulders with cold water. The initial cold shock response causes the heart rate to increase and breathing to become short and slightly laboured. All the while you should be concentrating on your breathing which then allows your body to overcome the initial shock. Once this has been done, proceed into the water at a controlled rate.

2. Walk in and immerse your whole body in the cold water – whilst not actually swimming but sitting in the water concentrating on your breathing to overcome the initial shock. Once you have your breathing and panic under control, then proceed onto the next stage – swimming. This would most likely be doing heads up front crawl or heads up breaststroke for a few minutes before you finally move onto full –i.e. head submerged – front crawl or breaststroke. Many do not even get to submerge their head.

3. Third and finally, you will always get the people who are too impatient for any of the above. They either dive in, if the option is available, or run into the water screaming something like, "FREEEEEEDDDOOOOMMM!!!!" before racing headlong into full immersion. Predictably there is one of two reactions: flailing around with a stroke rate of about a hundred strokes per minute to get themselves over the initial panic, or doing a swiftly

choreographed U-turn to only come racing out shouting various expletives at the top of their voice.

Either way, I am not one to say which is safer or a preferred method - but I have seen all of the above.

The next thing that will happen when in cold water is that your extremities will either experience a tingling effect or become numb. This is the result of vasoconstriction or constriction of the blood vessels, where blood is leaving your extremities and being pumped back to your core to protect your internal organs. At this point, you now need to focus on your breathing and keep it as deep as possible. Even when my extremities are numb, I will always periodically flex my hands, feet and move my fingers and toes to make sure that I still have cognitive control of them. Loss of dexterity in the limbs and disorientation starts occurring between 5 – 30 minutes after initial immersion. The numbness/tingly feeling can be either painful or exhilarating, or both, but stick with it and the results are amazing.

Now you are in the water and the blood has been diverted to your core, the sustained immersion results in your body temperature starting to drop. This can occur anywhere between 5 and 20 minutes of being in the water. Because it starts to drop so slowly you will still be in control as it occurs. The added exertion of swimming may help a bit to slow down the drop in body temperature.

After about 15 – 35 minutes you will start to feel very comfortable, as if a wave of warmth is engulfing your body. This is a further result of disorientation and deliriousness taking hold. This is the time that you should be getting out of the water. You are now getting hypothermic. Your body temperature would have dropped by a degree or two. Vasoconstriction in your extremities is keeping blood near your core.

So you get out of the water looking like a burnt lobster but feeling invigorated. You are not out of the danger zone yet. You now have about 5 minutes to get some warm clothes on before shivering will take hold of your body and your dexterity becomes seriously impaired. This is where your preparation pays off. Drinking a warm cup of coffee takes on a whole new meaning – if you manage to get it into your mouth without spilling it EVERYWHERE. You will very soon start to experience after drop. Now that you are out of the water and wrapped in something nice and warm, shivering away – this is a good thing. Your body does not react as quickly though so your body temperature will keep going down initially. This can last for anywhere up to 2 hours.

As your outer body and extremities have undergone vasoconstriction, it is imperative that you DO NOT warm the body up by getting into a boiling hot bath or shower. This can result in damaging your blood vessels by forcing blood out to the extremities too rapidly. Rather warm your body up slowly. In the 5 minutes straight after you get out, it is crucial to dry off as best you can, wrap up warm and get some warm liquids into your system. Whilst this is happening, it is a good idea not to do too much and just let your body equalise on its own. I generally cannot drive for about 30 – 40 minutes after I get out of the water as my feet are still pretty painful. I have been known to take about 2 – 3 hours to recover fully after a 20 minute dip in water between 1 and 4°C.

Another way in which people, especially those in the tropics can become acclimated to the cold, is to take cold showers or baths and for the more adventurous out there, you can even throw in a few blocks of ice. I know in South Africa, the local swimmers have an agreement with the local fishing community to create massive tubs of ice, into which they can jump and while the time away, sipping cocktails or reading their book. At least you do not have a shortage of ice for the cocktails ...Okay; I made the last bit up.

For all intents and purposes, there is really no need to go to the above lengths to prepare yourself for cold water swimming in the oceans and lakes unless you are specifically planning on swimming in the Arctic or Antarctic, or taking part in the fast growing ICE mile events. There is no real benefit to endurance swimming by submerging yourself in near freezing waters when the event you have planned will mostly likely be taking part in temperatures much closer to 14°C. Most endurance swimmers will steer clear of single digit temperatures, as we all must weigh up the makeup of our training. If you want to do the bigger distances in training, you are unlikely to sustain 6 hours swim in temperatures below 10°C.

A good reason for learning to deal with diverse temperatures is that it may not be the water that will be your nemesis, but rather the outside air. For example, you may swim at a time of the year where the water bodies have had a fair amount of the summer to warm up, and so are a nice tropical temperature. However, if you have a very chilly overcast night and the swim dictates that you swim some or all of the entire swim during the night, even if the daytime temperatures are decent, the night-time ones plummet. It is the outside temperature that can sap your energy and cause real issues with the cold. This effect becomes more apparent after you have been already swimming for 12 hours and you are feeling the effects of exertion - you now have to deal with the cold as your entire back of your body will be exposed to the elements.

Whichever way you choose to get used to the cold, make sure that you are never alone and to the best of your ability, make sure that it is in a controlled fashion. There is no need to do cold water training for the really extreme temperatures unless that is what you will be swimming in. If you have never done any cold water swimming, I would advise to go to an organised training session with people who know the signs of hypothermia and who will help gradually build you up to the longer distance. With this sport growing as quickly as it is, there are groups all over the country that are seasoned cold water swimmers. If it is the English Channel that you are aspiring to do, then the Dover harbour training is excellent to go to and they will over a relatively short period of time have you swimming in the harbour for a few hours at a time.

If the holy grail of cold water swimming, "The Ice Mile", is more your thing, again you will find groups globally that will help you with this challenge and get you to the point where a good half an hour in water that is 0°C will be like a walk in the park. You will experience the euphoria that cold water offers and also the "after-drop", and learn what it is like to have your skin on fire due to the cold and the buzz that it gives you. I would recommend everyone try it at some point as it teaches you a great deal about your physiology and how to cope with extreme environments. It is said that acclimatisation to the cold will stay with you for up to eighteen months before you will start to lose it.

DO NOT ATTEMPT TO DO ANY COLD WATER TRAINING ON YOUR OWN. I cannot emphasise this enough. Things can deteriorate pretty fast if not caught quickly, so prepare well, as the consequences can be severe. I have been at events where even the paramedics are not equipped to deal with people who have gone hypothermic, so make sure your event has adequate health and safety in place.

Chapter 13: Support Crew

As we all know, no person is an island and nothing in life happens solely by one person's efforts to achieve a goal. In all circumstances there are support crew ranging from family, loved ones and friends, to coaches and professionals such as doctors, nutritionists, physiotherapists, in some cases psychologists – and many more. All of these people are a vital part of any adventure or challenge. The people that you choose to surround yourself with are key, so take care to surround yourself with the RIGHT people - people that inspire you, challenge you, question your thought processes, and constantly keep you pushing the boundaries.

Whether these are paid for professionals or friends and family that just support you, it is a long and arduous road for all involved, especially for the immediate family of the person undertaking the challenge. Often, partners of the challenger are known as widows, and this is exactly what they become for the duration of the challenge, unless you are able to involve them in some way. Insane challenges are often undertaken by insane people (hence the need for psychologists along the way) and many of us are also slightly selfish with our time when we get into the zone and start the long journey from sofa to start line. This is totally understandable with the time that needs to be invested in making a challenge as much of a sure thing as is humanly possible. But be aware, your challenge may only last a year, and your relationships with people should last years and hopefully decades, so be extremely mindful of who you invite into your inner circle to assist you in any attempt.

When it comes to paying for a person's time, that is the easy part and there are plenty of people who will offer assistance and help you part with some hard-earned cash. There are a few things to think about when you are hiring coaches, doctors, physiotherapists and others. Vet them extensively - I normally go through word of mouth from people that I know are taking on the same or similar challenges. For instance, a personal trainer in a gym may be exceptional at getting people fit and getting them into more active lifestyle and more positive frame of mind. When it comes to taking on 10 plus hours of physical endurance, they may have no idea of what it takes. They could also be a huge liability when sitting on a boat for 15 – 30 hours in the channel due to sea sickness (mind you, this is true for all your crew). Nowadays, pilots are offering trial runs where you and your team can use their equipment and expertise for a couple of hours to get a feel of what it is like swimming near a boat in rough seas and your crew will be able to see how they are able to handle sea sickness. Be mindful that a massive ferry speeding across a stretch of rough water is TOTALLY different to a 30 – 50 foot boat pootling along at the speed of a swimmer, all the while getting buffeted by the wind and the waves.

If you do hire a personal coach with experience of endurance, they will become an invaluable asset not only in getting you physically into shape but also addressing some of the mental anguish that you might experience on your journey. Ultra-distance is a sport where the mental fortitude is far more important than physical aptitude. If your head is not in the right space, you are well on your way to failing so look very closely at your mental attitude and if you are able to get someone to help you with it, then do it. I have been lucky enough to be on and run some amazing personal development courses which luckily have helped me through. I truly believe the difference between success and failure (I really hate that word) is not governed by your physical wellbeing but your mental capability.

In reality, when taking on these events, few people take a professional to be with them on the boat when they undertake the event. For most, especially in the Channel crossing realm, where dates and times are not set in stone, support crew are usually made up of friends and family who are available at the time. In many circumstances, participants have their crew all lined up, but if their opportunity is affected by the weather gods – as is so often the case – then they have to accept anyone who can make themselves available at very short notice, as their primary support crew may not be able to be so flexible. In the ultra-distance swimming world, you will find that most people understand this and are very willing to help out when needed.

Let's take a look at the type of support that you will need on the day of your challenge(s). The bigger distances will require bigger input, for example, a Channel crossing will require you by law to have a motorised boat with crew and other forms of propulsion, i.e. a kayak or small motorised dinghy. Bear in mind that you could be on or with the boat for 20 plus hours. To hire a fully equipped boat for that amount of time does not come cheap, but then you are generally getting a fully equipped boat, its crew, captain and fuel so if you break it down to a per hour cost, it is not that expensive.

Once you have hired the boat, then it is generally up to you to provide your own crew. These are the people you want on the boat to kick your backside, offer positive inspirational support and feed you, and for all of this they will generally get your more ugly side – believe me, endurance athletes can be REALLY grumpy when things are getting tough. This is the reason why the people you have with you are extremely important. Often, some pilots are not happy to have family members on board, especially parents, wives, husbands and the like. Often, the emotional turmoil involved when their loved one is going through what can be some very rough patches is not easy to deal with, especially when there is very little they can do to help. This is where friends are best as they generally do not have the same emotional attachments to the athlete. On the other hand, most athletes want their loved ones on board - I was adamant that I wanted my parents and family on the boat and I stuck to my original swim slot specifically for this reason. Nearly everything my brother and I had done while growing up had been done with my parents around, supporting us in various ways. Both my brother and I were world class sailors, but my parents never sailed. They had spent most their life following their kids around and I wanted this to be no different. Retrospectively,

I think my mother was a nervous wreck at the start. By the end, she was an emotional shell having just watched her little baby (okay, a 100kgs of hulking hippo – but her baby all the same) going through some very emotional meltdowns. It didn't help that she was not really that good on a boat that was being tossed around by the elements. Fortunately, they would not have had it any other way and I would not have either, but it can be very hard watching a loved one have an emotional meltdown.

Often, on longer Channel swims, the swimmer may want a buddy swimmer, someone who is able to swim with the swimmer for short periods. In Channel swims, the rules and regulations that go with these buddy swimmers are that they are not allowed to swim with the swimmer in the first four hours and then when they can swim with them, they only go in for an hour at a time. They are not allowed to pace the challenger so will have to swim either beside or behind them but not ahead. Once the hour is up, they will not be allowed in again for another three hours. For this I had two, Pygmy hippo (my brother) and Greg Woods, the aforementioned fellow Channel swimmer that I met whilst training. Greg had done his crossing two weeks before mine and, with his recent experience, he was an invaluable person to have on the boat with me.

On any boat, there needs to be a chain of command and the captain needs to be informed as to who does what and who is responsible for what when things start to get tough. Generally, the call to end a swim is with the captain of the boat, being the most experienced, but this is a last resort, and each person has to be responsible for some part of the support. An observer is always provided by the governing body whose primary role is to observe and catalogue the swim, to make sure it is all legal and can be later ratified as a successful swim. In my support crew, Spencer was my chief support, whose role was to provide feeds, keep up morale and be a buddy swimmer. My wife at the time, Rachelle, was in charge of preparing feeds, giving reassurance and social media management. Ultimately, it is far better to have two or three suitable people on a boat as support crew than ten of your mates.

For lake swims, the rules are different and vary depending on where you are in the world. At least lake swims are more predictable in that they can be organised on a specific day, making planning far easier than sitting around, sometimes for weeks on end, hoping that the weather will play nicely. Comparatively, a lot of the iconic ocean swims (English Channel, Catalina Channel, Tsugaru Channel, Cook Straits – to mention a few) attract swimmers from around the globe and often you can fly halfway around the globe, sit around for two to three weeks and not even get to swim.

For support, lake swims generally only require a kayaker, but for the longer distances, a small motorised boat with a secondary form of propulsion is needed, with two or more support crew. I think in many circumstances, these swims are harder on the support crew than they are on the athlete. All the athlete has to do is keep going, just keep swimming. The poor kayaker is responsible for being physically fit for kayaking, navigating, inspiring, feeding the athlete (as well as themselves) photography, social media management, and if that is not enough, they sometimes have to sit in the pouring rain for ten plus hours, being at the receiving end of the athlete's tantrums, being responsible for their physical wellbeing. Believe me, it is far easier doing the challenge than it is supporting it - so yes, they are the most under-appreciated part of any marathon swim team. In my team I have the Zimhippo – me, the swimmer and Slimhippo, my adorable wife. It is an amazing way to take on challenges as a couple but the same pitfalls that you can have in bigger events still ring very true in lake swims with regards to emotional turmoil.

With any form of support, there are always logistics involved in how the support will be carried out. At the beginning of an event, the athlete and the support crew need to be in agreement of exactly how feeding and sustaining an athlete is going to be carried out, for example with charts and feeding logs and types of energy drinks and bars, how many to have and when to give them. What is often not taken into account is, what happens if circumstances unfold where the initial plan has to be shelved? In other words, what is plan B, C and sometimes D?

An example of this was a seventeen-mile swim in Arizona where we experienced head winds in excess of 25 miles per hour (mph), for the majority of the swim. This is fine if you are the swimmer in the water with very little wind resistance, but if you are a kayaker, on a sit-on-top kayak, with your entire body and kayak acting as a sail, things can get challenging very quickly. Every time the Slimhippo stopped kayaking she just disappeared backwards, hence she could not feed me properly. After four hours of fighting against the wind and her not being able to feed herself, she was struggling to keep up with me. The organisers then stepped in and dragged her about one kilometre ahead of me so that I would swim and meet them drifting back. All good, I hear you say; well, in dragging her forward, she got completely soaked. Again, we went through the whole process of her trying to keep up with me and feed me. Being in wet clothes and subject to winds of 25mph brings on another problem - the Slimhippo does not have the luxury of being clinically obese with a generous layer of bioprene to keep her nice and warm. I was about to suggest to the organiser that I tow her; yes, tie a rope around my waist and I tow her when she cannot kayak, so as not to lose each other! However, they dragged her forward once again. This time they deposited her in a little sheltered crevice amongst the rocks to wait for me. Now that she was wet, cold and not expending any energy, it did not take long for her to feel the effects of the elements IN ARIZONA of all places and be unable to continue. This now left me in a dilemma. I was now in the territory of having to abandon my swim, as normally in these circumstances, if you lose your support crew, your swim is over. Luckily, I talked with the organiser who knew my ability, and thankfully let me carry on with another swimmer and their kayaker. This however created its own issues as the kayaker now had to support two swimmers of very different abilities. As the swimmer tagging along, you are totally obliged to stay with that kayaker even if they are slower. This brought on another complication - I was not swimming fast enough to generate sufficient body heat to keep warm. Finally I was told that we had about 1.5km left so I talked to the organisers again and asked if I could leave that kayaker and just make my way to the finish line on my own, as I really needed to put some pace into my limbs. They were happy with that so, with full afterburners engaged, I sprinted to the end. It was great to get some heat back into my body.

PLANNING! PLANNING! PLANNING! Another time I realised the importance of planning was Loch Lomond, when my support crew had to scrap plan A and devise plans B, C and D on the go. You can NEVER do enough planning and even when you think you have all bases covered, things can still go wrong. When they do go wrong, having the right crew is ESSENTIAL.

Colleen Blair (Land crew and Amazing cold and ultra distance swimmer). Spencer Schlachter (AKA Pygmy Hippo) Zimhippo and Audra (AKA Slimhippo). For one lake swim (Loch Lomond), this was my core crew plus Robert Hamilton and Stewart Griffiths who I hired the boat from.

On the lake and smaller swims, it is crucial to make sure you know – as best you can, what sort of vessel you will be using to crew as all vessels are not equal. Most commonly on the swims where the organisers offer a vessel as part of the swim, it is usually a sit-on-top kayak. These are easy to use, and generally people with little ability can use them, but they do have a downside in that you are effectively sitting on top

194

of the craft offering your body as further wind resistance. They do generally have easy places to store kit, but just be aware of the wind resistance problem. Another concern with these craft is that they are not very watertight so expect to have a wet bum for pretty much most of the journey.

Another option that sometimes is available is the sea kayak. These are much better when it comes to dealing with waves on an open lake and some will have a skirt that will clip onto the top of the vessel whilst you are cocooned by the craft. The one downside with these vessels is, as you are inside the vessel, most your kit will also have to be inside and getting to essential equipment can be a lot more onerous. There is generally little space on top of the vessel to strap everything outside and accessibility to equipment strapped on may be limited, as you have far less space to move about the craft so planning your packing is crucial.

Slimhippo in Lago D Orta Italy. – As support she sat in the kayak for 8 hours feeding and looking after me.

Paddle boards are another great option, especially if the water is flat, but add in any form of headwind and things become very tricky very quickly, as like the sit-on-tops, your entire body acts as wind resistance. These are not commonly offered by organisers when booking swims, but people occasionally bring them with as they are fairly portable, often fitting into their own bag so can probably be taken on an aircraft with you. An additional downside to these is that there is very little in the form of fastening points to strap stuff to. This can be circumvented by all sorts of contraptions where you tow an inflatable tube to store stuff on but, in my opinion, these are more hassle than they are worth.

Other acceptable craft include canoes or row boats and these can often take up to three people. This is a requirement on some of the longer overnight swims where one support crew is needed to do the rowing while the others will be in charge of taking care of the swimmer. This is has the added advantage of giving the support crew some company. There is usually very little cover on these canoes so if there is any precipitation in the air, your crew will be wet for most of the swim. On some swims, electrically powered boats are available. Generally, these will take up to three people and often have a covered area where the crew can shelter should the weather become inclement. One downfall of these craft is the length of the charge on the battery. Once that goes you are reduced to oar power. This is not always acceptable by the organisers so be sure to check with them first, if this is your craft of choice.

Last but not least, land crew may be required for some of the longer colder lake swims, where there are several swimmers of differing abilities and only one or two health and safety craft to support all entrants. Your shore crew should consist of one or two people that follow your progress along the shoreline, who are ready to provide ongoing support should you have to be rescued and transported to the closest shore by the health and safety boat. They take over responsibility for you at that point. It is very important to have the right people for this as well, and for Loch Lomond it did not come any better than the queen of Scottish swimming, Colleen Blair. We were very grateful to have Colleen, as she not only gave up her entire Saturday night to drive (very slowly!) down the length of the loch to support us, but also thought of and provided all the things that we hadn't even considered important, like flasks, even warmer clothing than what we had and the bug spray!! We were fortunate enough to have met Colleen and her amazing family in Arizona three years previously, when we were a part of the SCAR swim together. It really tells you something about the calibre of the swimming community and its supportive nature when you have greats such as Colleen and also many others that have helped us along the way, willing to give of their time and knowledge to help you succeed.

If you are travelling internationally, it is essential to take a few things with you. Below is a list of useful things that can come in very handy:

- **Buoyancy aid** - Some organisers may give them to you but not all, so it can be a useful thing to have.
- **Gloves -** If you end up being offered a kayak or a canoe, I would suggest two pairs. One with padded palms and cut off fingers similar to cycling or sailing gloves. The cut off finger or fingers still offer you full dexterity. The other pair is a warmer pair should the weather be cold and wet. Another useful thing to keep handy is heat packs for gloves especially for the colder swims and for overnight, as you can chemically activate them and put them in your gloves.

- **Bungee cords** – to strap stuff onto the kayak or canoe and help you store stuff.
- **Carabiners** to attach things to the bungee cords or kayak.
- **Safety pins** to tie lights and lighter stuff to the bungee cords or kayak itself.
- **Something comfortable to sit on** - a pair of wetsuit shorts works well, but if you are the Slimhippo, she uses my crochet shorts as a cushion. I like to have them at the end of a swim but by the time I get them, they are usually soaked.
- **Headlights and torches** - headlights are a lot easier to handle as you have you hands free to be doing other things.
- **Food** – its not a good idea to experiment with snack foods in a foreign country, so where possible, it may be helpful to take your own. Flasks are useful for the cold and for night swims.
- **Waterproof bags** are useful to keep stuff dry. It is useful to get a waterproof cover for your phone that has a clear front that you can still use the phone.
- **For the ladies, a way to go to the loo** - a G-whizz or a She-wee can be very useful to aid in relieving yourself. Another option is adult diapers. Otherwise, just keep close to the shore and when you need to just pop onshore.

- **Hats, sun creams, sunglasses and layers** so that you can get warm if needed and also take stuff off if needed. A lot can happen to the weather in 15 hours.
- **Bug spray and a hat net** where midges or mosquitoes can be problematic.

Other items may be required to have depending on the organising body. They may or may not provide them or even require them, so it can be useful to have them with you:

- **Alpha Flag -** flown to let other watercraft that there is a swimmer in the water.
- **Lights** - commonly used when swims may end up going into the night or take place through the night. For the swimmer, you will need a flashing light usually placed on the head of the swimmer, and another on the back of the costume.
- **GPS tracker –** not a necessity but nice for your followers to be able to monitor your progress.
- **Whistle or extra form of communication –** this is just in case your technology lets you down!

Chapter 14: Success or Not?

In any journey that you take in your life, there will always be an opportunity to learn. There will also be an instance when things do not go according to plan, or you were *not successful* (notice the wording that I have used again). Some of you might class being unsuccessful as FAILURE. If it were up to me, I would banish that word from the English language. It, and the way we are made to believe *not succeeding* is a terrible thing, is associated with so much negativity. Like I mentioned earlier, words are powerful things, use them carefully.

Have I ever failed at anything I have done? The answer is *no*. I have however *not been successful* on numerous occasions, too many to count, and in many areas of my life. Every single one of those occasions has led to a huge learning opportunity. In all my open water swims, yes, I do have a GOAL in mind, generally the big swim I am leading up to. But as this is a journey rather than a single goal, every swim to me is regarded as a training swim, affording me the ability to learn, while simultaneously adding to the amount of knowledge that I can take away from the experience.

In every goal that I attempt to achieve, I generally try to adopt a completely new preparation regime, based on what I already know, to test my ability of what I can and what I cannot do. The only unsuccessful swim I have had to date is the Champion of Champions down in Dover. The format is as follows: 5 mile followed by a 3 mile, followed by a 1 mile swim. There is a time limit on each of the swims, so if you are relatively quick you get to have a rest in between each of them. I had trained in 10°C water and was comfortable that I could do 5 miles without any food, then fuel up and get dry and warm for the next one. However, with open water you are reliant on other factors such as tides, weather, moving buoys and many other things. On this particular swim, it is very difficult to place a buoy in Dover harbour and keep it there for any length of time, unless you have the ability to tether it to a fixed point on the sea floor. The day I did it, the water was a lot colder than expected, at about 11°C. Even from the start, there was confusion as to whether we would be doing 1 km laps or 500m laps.

The race got underway, all was going well, and we came up to the point in time when I figured I had done my 5 miles. I swam another lap just to be on the safe side. I then asked the officials how many more laps I had left and they mentioned I had another four laps to do. I was a bit surprised as I had been going for my expected time plus, and still had another 4km to go. I carried on. After what I thought was four laps, I was heading to the shore only to be chased down and told I had to do another lap. This was bonkers! I was now very cold as I had been in the water for over three hours without any feeds. By the time I got out, I could not walk and just curled up in a ball when I dragged myself out of the water. I was blue and did not have the ability to shiver at first even though I was frozen. I had gone hypothermic. I was assisted up the beach and I began the slow process of getting warm. I was then told that the 5 mile had actually turned into an 8.6 mile swim!

So what did I learn? I had previously learnt in my long-distance swimming that with regards to distance, I can easily surpass the mental safeguards that my mind imposes. I now learnt that I could spend nearly 1.5 hours longer than I had ever planned in water of that temperature. It was a good lesson in how far you can go over your mentally imposed barriers. I did not manage to finish the overall challenge, but the information I took away was a massive boost in my overall self-esteem.

Another time I tried testing my barriers, was with Lago D'Orta, a 28km lake swim in Italy. I had been chatting to a friend of mine who kept their training to a minimum but had been doing it very regularly. I figured I would try this out. I would prepare for this with swims no longer than 90 minutes (about 5 -7km) and I would not do any swims longer than that apart from the two other events that I had entered, both around the 10km mark, so about 2 hours 30 to 2 hours 45 minutes about 6 weeks and 4 weeks prior to the event. Other than that, I was doing 90 minutes three times a week. For the distance side of things, I elected to rely entirely on my mental preparation. I knew I could and had done the distance in the past so that was a big plus for my mind. For the 90 minute swims I adopted my usual training protocol - total body confusion, negative splits, active rest and high intensity.

The swim took place and I was successful. The jump from 90 minutes of swimming to just over 8 hours is a *huge* jump. It was an experiment on my part. I got through it successfully and finished in the medals but the lesson I took away was that I would never advocate that sort of training for a swim of 20km plus. It did prove again how powerful the mind is to get me through it. A full article about it exists on my website.

My attitude and outlook to any challenge is that I have a 50% chance of succeeding or not. Those odds never change for any of us. The other thing that keeps me going is that if people have done it before, there is no reason that I cannot do it. The next step is to move those goals more in my favour and even if the movement is slight, it is still in my favour and the rest is left in the lap of the gods. I choose to keep my physical training minimal, based on past experiences, both good and bad, and to help mitigate repetitive type injuries before I get to the start. I am certain that there will be challenges in my future that will find me wanting and I relish the thoughts of those - another opportunity to learn! One aspect I will not forgo on is my daily mental routine. This covers not only my swimming but every aspect of my life.

Chapter 15: A challenge summary

In any goal, whether it has been in the making for a few months or a few years, the time will come when you have to stop talking about it and actually do it. This comes with a completely new set of emotions and the following is a summary of my swim across the English Channel.

I was lucky to have been called up for my swim over a weekend. I also had the misfortune of having the most horrendous cough which I had picked up a few days previously. I knew that this was the last opportunity to do this swim this year, so I could not really delay it any longer. It was a spring tide and I figured that I would go to Dover anyway. As it was nearing the close of the season, there were only about three swimmers down for the weekend training. If I were to do this all again, I would do it a lot earlier in the season! At the first weekend there had been about 50 swimmers and now there were two. We were both aiming to head across to France in the next day or two.

I was very concerned when I went in to do a 2 hour swim as I had been unable to swim more than about 200m in the last two days without having a huge coughing fit before I could carry on. This day was no different. I swam about 500m then spent the next minute or two coughing up a lung before I could swim again. This lasted for about an hour. My nose was just streaming for most of the swim. I was now very concerned; it was going be interesting trying to swim to

France like that! Amazingly, the saltwater cured me, and by the end of the swim I was able to swim without coughing at all. I do not know how it happened, but I was now cough free and my nose had run itself out.

I then got a call from Alison Streeter to say we would be leaving Dover harbour at 10 am the following morning. There was a lot to do! I had to let my support crew know we were on, get my parents and crew down to Dover and bring the kit that I needed. I had to plan and prepare all my feeds and the food for the crew on board. As it was the weekend, the word spread amongst my friends that I would be swimming to France on Sunday morning. Quite a few of them decided to ditch their plans and come down to Dover on Saturday night for a few drinks. Not something I was really in the mood for, so I decided to have dinner with them then head off for an early night – well, so I thought. Final preparations were made to my feed and feeding plan, final packing was done, and I went to bed for a good night sleep. My mind however had a different idea on how to prepare for what was the biggest physical challenge I had ever taken on.

After tossing and turning most of the night, wide awake, it was about 4.30am when I decided I had to go and do something. I went out of the hotel for a nice long walk along the promenade and the pier and onto the White Cliffs of Dover. I took some time to sit and watch the sunrise over the ocean and reflect on the day ahead. Sleep was the furthest thing from my mind. Fortunately, my cough from the previous day had completely disappeared so I sat on the cliffs taking in the views and the calm and reflecting on how privileged I was to be embarking on such an amazing adventure. Emotion overtook me while I just sat and absorbed everything about the day ahead.

By the time I got back to the hotel, more friends started arriving from around the country. We sat and had some breakfast (except I was only really eating because I had to - I really did not feel like eating at all). Although I had a huge amount of friends around, none of whom had ever seen or known someone stupid enough to swim to France, amidst the banter and offers of a ferry ticket, I was jovial but totally aloof while I got ready for the short trip to the harbour to meet up with Alison on her Boat Roco. When she saw me, my entourage and our kit, she asked if we were going for a week as we had come totally over prepared. All too soon I was saying goodbye to my friends and I jumped on the boat with my team for the journey to the start. My parents were wrapped up as if we were going to the Arctic and I was in my usual t-shirt and shorts. On the journey to Samphire Hoe, I busied myself with the paperwork of the swim to come and went over my feeding plan with the observer and Alison. Alison was also giving me some last-minute advice, and one piece rang loud and clear ... it was, if you put a polystyrene cup in the water here, at some point it will arrive in France.

In no time at all it was time for me to get ready, I got changed into my costume and my brother got the unenviable task of greasing me up. The answer to the most commonly asked question of a channel swimmer is NO, I do not use goose fat. I use Vaseline for all areas that are prone to chafing - under my arms, on the front of my shoulders so I do not dig a hole into them with my stubble, and around the back of my neck. I donned the gloves to lather my groin area in Vaseline. A stick light was attached to the back of my costume and one to the back of my goggles. I was now ready.

As the boat stopped about 100m from the shoreline at the end of Samphire Hoe, Alison came above deck to finalise the administrative stuff with me and get me on my way. There were 2 other boats with swimmers ready to start and one that had already struck out for French shores. Final instructions were given - swim to the shore, get out of the water entirely, signal to the boat when I was ready, and then I would start. After saying my final goodbyes to my family and a few photo opportunities, I entered the water. It was about 16°C - you never get over the initial shock of getting into cold water! I took a few moments to control my breathing, and then I was off to the beach.

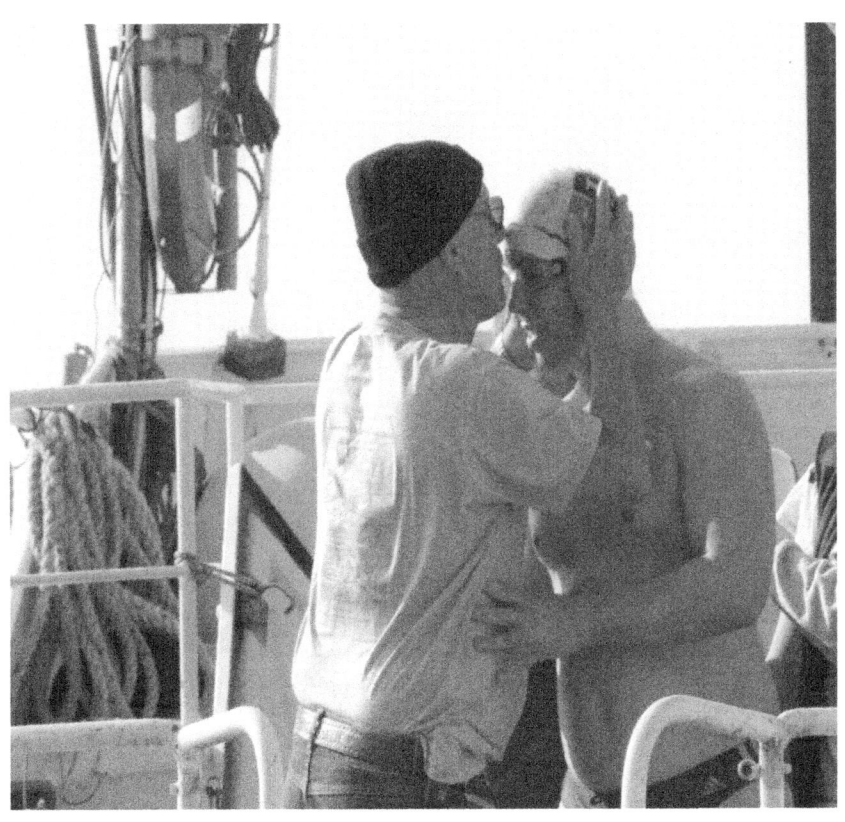

God Bless my son. Swim well

Mama and Papa Hippo with Zimhippo

I stumbled my way up the shore and greeted my friends. After hellos and thanks and then goodbyes, I signalled to Alison that I was ready. The horn went at 10am and I made my way back into the ocean, followed shortly by my well-wishing friend Doug Robinson, who thought it would be a good idea to strip down to his smalls and swim to France with me. He lasted all of about 50 metres before stopping and turning back. I heard later that he'd come out of the water swearing about how cold the water was!

I was finally off. The first two hours were pretty fast with a stroke rate of 68 strokes per minute. I had opted for my first

210

feed to be at 2 hours, a great opportunity to put my head down, generate some body heat, and put some distance between me and the white cliffs of Dover. Although it was a spring tide, the weather was great and the water pretty flat, so I was able to really get into a comfortable stroke. All systems were working perfectly. My focus was intently on my stroke, keeping it as long and as relaxed as I could. Focus on the finger drag, hand entry as far in front as possible, not lift my arms too high out of the water, keep my head down, do not breathe too high, my mantra playing nicely in my head, just keep swimming, just keep swimming, just keep swimming. It was a great start and emotions came over me in waves. How lucky I was to have this opportunity! How lucky I was to have friends who wanted to be part of this adventure. How lucky I was that I had somehow taken my abused body from the state it was in eight months previously to a point where even I believed I could do something like this. But the biggest euphoria came from the thought that on that boat were my parents. I had them to thank for my sheer existence and the chance to make them proud of me brought tears to my eyes.

It was time for my first feed. I stopped and looked for the boats that had left with me. They were dropping back with their swimmers and I had made significant gains on the boat and swimmer that had left ahead of me. I then looked back – stupid thing to do! The White Cliffs loomed as large as they had two hours ago. It was like I had gone nowhere in the last two hours. Oh well, I was here, so best not complain. I took on my food as quickly as I could and got back to the task at hand. My stroke rate had slowed to about 64 strokes per minute, but I was still feeling comfortable. Knowing I had a long way to go, I kept it at the slower rate. I then found something else to focus on which elated me - I needed to pee. This was a good sign as being able to pee is a indication that my internal systems were working well. It takes a lot of concentration for me to pee in open water, so I spent a fair amount of time coaxing my bladder to relieve itself. The day progressed - 3 hours, then 4 hours. Those bloody cliffs seemed to NEVER disappear. It was at this point that I asked for a buddy swimmer, and Greg donned his kit and came in to join me for an hour. The weather was changing slightly, and the wind was picking up and was now about force 3, but the wind was going with the waves so the sea was not lumpy at all. The waves were long, so I was able to keep my stroke together. You get a few different scenarios in the ocean and I was happy that the wind was moving in the same direction as the waves, resulting in very long, generally flat waves. The alternative is when the wind is going opposite to the waves causing them to get very choppy and the ocean to get quite lumpy as the opposing forces work against each other. At hour 5, Greg got out and I was back on my own. We were in the English Shipping zone and we could now start to see the ships ploughing their way through the channel. It was a surreal experience seeing a massive container ship pass, and then about 5 minutes later be hit by the wake of that boat.

The Channel has specific zones for traffic. The Inshore Traffic Zone from the Dover shore stretches about 5 nautical miles towards France before becoming the South West Shipping Lane, which is about 4 nautical miles across. In this lane, ships will be travelling from the south west. You then have about 1 nautical mile in the middle of the Channel known as the Separation Zone. The North East Shipping Lane then extends for about 4 nautical miles towards France, where the ships will be travelling in a north easterly direction. Finally, you get the French Inshore Traffic Zone. So, it is a bit like a motorway through the channel with the Separation Zone being the central reservation. About 500 ships plough through these lanes in a 24-hour period, while a plethora of other craft (Channel crossing pilot boats being in that group) cross from England to France.

After 6 hours my stroke rate was still at 64 and all systems were running smoothly, but those bloody cliffs were still there - albeit they were getting smaller. The wind had stayed pretty much the same and I had seen quite a few jellyfish, but in my head we had come to an agreement that they would be happy for me to share their water with them for the day, and it seemed that they had picked up on this agreement and were happy to stick to the contract. I did not bother them and they did not bother me. We were soon in the Separation Zone and I could now see ships coming from my left and my right-hand side, and they were not getting any smaller. My crew were mostly enjoying themselves - although my mother had been feeding the fish and we nearly lost my father over the edge when Roco was hit by the wake from a passing boat. My father was on a deck chair on the top deck whilst my brother was sleeping/dozing on one of the fitted benches. When the wake hit and Roco lurched to starboard, my father started his journey across the top deck, only to be slammed into the railings before the boat lurched to port and commenced my father's journey in the opposite direction across the boat. My brother woke to see our father sliding across the deck and managed to catch him before he hit the opposite railing.

Not having a watch on and not knowing how far I had gone and how far was left, it was a good sign to see the sun starting to set, so I did the maths in my head and figured I had been swimming for about 8 hours. This was a huge point for me as I was now entering into unknown territory, as 8 hours was the longest I had ever swum. This played havoc with my mind and I hit the proverbial wall about twenty minutes later. I stopped and switched into breaststroke and broke down in tears. The boat slowed and went across me so I could swim on the other side of it and it could protect me from the waves. My brother came to the back of the boat to ask if the diesel fumes were getting to me. I just shouted back at him, "Everything IS FUCKING GETTING TO ME!" After faffing around for a few minutes and my team talking me through this meltdown, I got back to the task at hand while they watched the sunset.

Being so late in the season, I now had another challenge to deal with. The nights were getting colder and the outside air temperature soon dropped to below what the water temperature was. As I had my whole back exposed to the frigid air temperatures, the challenge was not to keep warm in the water, but to try not let the outside air take its toll. At the next feed, and after my mental meltdown, the team figured it was time to put another swimmer in the water with me for an hour to lift my spirits. The Pygmy hippo dived in near me and soon the two brothers were in the water together. This was an extremely proud moment for me to swim with my brother – the man who I blame/commend for sowing a seed about this barmy sport 9 months earlier. Once my brother left, I was on my own again. My body was fine, I was taking on food, and I was peeing regularly. My tongue was swollen and my back was aching a bit. My mind however was now frail, and the doubts kept rearing their ugly head over and over again. My focus now was not on my body but keeping the demons at bay.

My mind drifted back to the many times that I had swum in the harbour and an amazing paraplegic friend, Ros Hardiman, who forced me to ask myself, "If she has the fortitude to carry on, then there is no reason for me NOT to!" Another question that had to be answered over and over again was: "Is my mind just bored or am I physically not able to carry on?" If the answer was the former, then put your head down and swim. It was one of the biggest mental battles I had ever had to fight - to the extent that the rest of my body was now in automatic mode. I cared nothing about the pain in my back or my groin. All I focused on was the battle in my head. Then another thought popped into my head: my parents had *not* flown halfway around the globe and put most of their holiday on hold to watch me get out halfway across. I would not be the one to have wasted their time and the time of my crew.

Friends can be an amazing bunch but coming from Africa, friends can be a bit different. There was always a good dose of banter between us - sometimes this could get very cutting. In my head I figured that I had two choices and their consequences. They were as follows: If I get to France, I will go back a Channel swimmer, and there would be much Joy and praise from them. I would recover pretty quickly and get back to my life. However, if I did not get to France, the banter and mental anguish that I would have to endure for years to come as being the guy that NEARLY swam to France was more tortuous than actually getting there. Luckily, I will never have to find out if I would still be being tormented by them today. I found it quite interesting to learn what keeps you going in times of distress.

My brother, now being back on the boat and after one feed had come to the back of the boat and mentioned to me that we could see the lights of France. My response was, "You can see the fucking lights of France from Dover on a clear day!" He was just trying to help because he knew that I would want an idea of where I was.

I was starting to lose focus and I really needed something to pick me up. There is an unwritten rule in Channel swimming - NEVER let the swimmer know how far you have to go or how far you have come. There is a reason for this and it is geographical. The narrowest part of the English Channel is between Dover on the United Kingdom coast and Cap Gris-Nez on the French Coast. At that point there is the Cap Gris-Nez Lighthouse, perched on top of the Cliff. Both north and south of this point the French coast gets further away from the UK, resulting in a greater distance from Dover. Couple this with the fact that the tides run furiously through that 21 mile stretch, especially the spring tides, and you can end up in a situation where you are travelling parallel to the coast, even though said coast may only be a mile away. If you are not swimming fast enough to make headway across the tides, you are left with one option, to swim another 5 or 6 hours until the tide turns and drops you back onto the shore.

At 10 hours in, my stroke rate was still pretty constant at around 64 strokes per minute. My mother was still feeding the fish and my team were prepping for my next feed. I was soon called for a feed and I was now on to the double strength Maxim™ again to give me extra energy. Actually, I think it was more like triple strength. I had long since stopped taking on solid food as the whole of my mouth inside had swelled up due to the salt. It was pitch dark and I could see the light house of Cap Gris-Nez. I was told that I had to push hard for a bit as the tide was turning and I really needed to up my speed. The lighthouse was on my left, so I figured that it was in the right place. In reality I had no idea. I thought this is where all the negative splitting in my training would come in handy. Time to give it my all!

I then took on a feed at about 11 hours 15 minutes. My pace had gone up to about 68 strokes per minute. The mood on the boat was a little bit more subdued. Understandable as it is not easy being on a boat travelling so slowly for that long being thrown about by the Channel. Cap Gris-Nez was now on my right, so the tide had turned. Now I had a dread in my mind. Bearing in mind that all I could see was the flashing light of the Lighthouse, all the things I knew about fast tides, swimming parallel to France for 5 hours, not making headway across the tide, came to haunt me. The tide was now running back along the coast, so worst case scenario I would be washed past the Cap and end up in Calais. I was preparing my mind for another 4 -5 hours in the Channel. This was a massive emotional downer. I was cursing myself for letting this happen. Chastising myself for not swimming faster, not training harder, wasting so much time at feeds and many other negative thoughts with the realisation that I MIGHT have missed the Cap. My heart sank. But Alison stopped me briefly and told me that if I really up my pace, I could make shore in the next 30 – 40 minutes. I could see absolutely nothing, just the flashing of the lighthouse. Well, time to either finish this swim or break myself doing it! Off I went at what I felt was a blistering pace. Determined that I was **not** going to have another feed, I gave it all I could. After about 35 minutes, I stopped the boat and told them that they needed to tell me if I was going to make it because there was no way I could keep this pace up for much longer. I was told that my stroke rate had gone up to 74. Then they brought out a spotlight and shone it towards the lighthouse, and in the gloom, I could make out the jagged rocks of the French coast. They said, "Go and get your Channel swim and your French pebble!"

It is customary that when you have swum the channel that you pick up a pebble and put it in your trunks to take home for keepsakes.

With renewed vigour, I headed to the rocks. As I would be landing on the rocks, for safety reasons, they put both Pygmy Hippo and Greg back in the water to swim with me to the end. Now I could definitely see nothing - not only was it pitch black, but I burst into tears as I swam the last 200m to the rocks. My hand brushed against the rocks and I tried to put my feet down, but it was a big submerged boulder so I put my feet down then promptly walked about a metre before falling off the submerged rock back into the ocean. I swam again until I felt another rock, this time I crawled along this one until I fell off the edge of it, cutting myself in the process. I swam again and every boulder I got to took me closer to the sheer rock face. Soon I found one I could stand on but the water was still lapping over it so my feet were getting wet. It was time to crawl off this rock in search of another that was higher up. After clambering over a few more, I finally found one that I could stand on without water lapping over my feet. I climbed onto it from the water with Greg and Pygmy Hippo in close proximity to stop me falling off. You cannot conceive how hard it is to stand up after swimming for that long. The spotlight then shone on me to see I was out and the horn blew.

Proud Mum and buggered son.

IT WAS OVER!!! I had become the 1012th person to cross the English Channel and I just sat on the rocks crying. The emotion just overwhelmed me and it took a while for me to compose myself enough to gingerly get back into the Channel and negotiate my way out to deeper water where I had to traverse the hundred odd metres back to the boat. Sadly, I did not get my pebble from France. My trunks would have had to be considerably larger to get one of those boulders that I had been stumbling over into them! The swim to the boat seemed to take ages, swimming with Greg and my brother. When I reached the boat I thought I had left all my emotional tears on the shoreline but as I boarded that boat and looked up to see my mother, wife and father all in tears, well, I could contain myself no longer and the water works started again. As I reached the top of the ladder, my father was there to give me the longest hug. In my father's embrace and amongst the tears all he could bring himself to say was, "It's like hugging a bloody ice block! I am so proud of you my son." It took us all a while to compose ourselves enough for me to get some photos for posterity, thank everyone on the boat for their amazing work and make my way below deck to get changed. I took two steps down into the boat and immediately had to turn around and head for the side to vomit up all the energy drink that had not been utilised. The thought occurred to me to come fishing here one day as there must be some seriously big fish on this stretch of water due to all the excess energy drink in it.

I soon learnt that I had done the Channel swim in 11 hours 45 minutes. All except one of us was ecstatic with my time. This would be Greg Woods – my training partner and good friend. He had swum the channel fourteen days earlier in a phenomenal time of 11 hours 51 minutes. Before my swim, I thought there was no way I was going to better that, but it did give me a loose idea of what time I MIGHT expect. He was gutted that I had beat him. I heard that he had mentioned to Alison that if I beat his time he will swim back to France. For whatever reason, this did not happen - but our friendly rivalry continues to this day, ten years later. Secretly, he is a better swimmer than me – just not in the Channel! Thank you Greg, for being such a great friend and great sport. I also learnt that of the four swimmers that left on the 28th September and the four that left on the 27th of September, I was the only one who had successfully managed to get to France.

The Channel Swimming & Piloting Federation

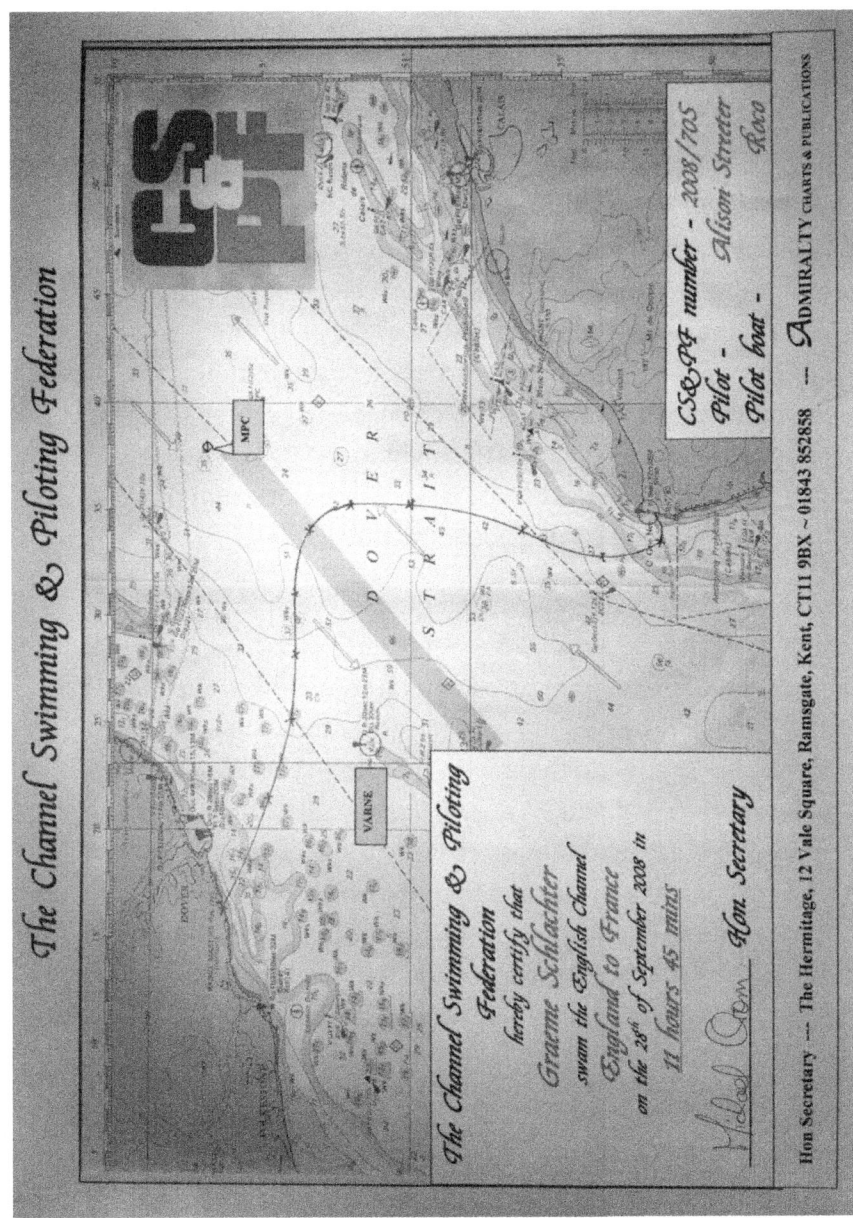

CS&PF

The Channel Swimming & Piloting Federation

hereby certify that

Graeme Schlachter

swam the English Channel

England to France

on the 26th of September 2008 in

11 hours 45 mins

Hon Secretary

CS&PF number - 2008/705
Pilot - Alison Streeter
Pilot boat - Roco

Hon Secretary — The Hermitage, 12 Vale Square, Ramsgate, Kent, CT11 9BX ~ 01843 852858 — ADMIRALTY CHARTS & PUBLICATIONS

When I show people my track across to France I am often asked how far I swam in distance as I got pushed way up the channel and back in a large "n" shape. The answer is I left from Dover and I landed directly under the Cap so I swam the shortest route of 21 miles. I did not swim 28 or 32 or 45. You swim between where you start and when you end, the curves in the plot are solely due to current and generally negate themselves so if you get washed to the right for 6 hours then left for the next 6 hours, you have not swum that distance, the tide has carried you in that direction.

It was time to wrap up and get a bit of shut eye during the 3 hour journey back to Dover. At around 3am, we pulled into the port and there to greet us was about ten of the group of friends that had watched me start my adventure about 16 hours earlier. They were there with champagne and crystal glasses that they had bought during the day. Also there to greet us was the legend that is Freda. After docking and unpacking the boat, it was time for me to head back to London. I left my parents in Dover in the hotel as they were off on a trip of their own the following day, my friends made their way home and my brother, wife and I headed back home at about 5 am.

I got home and slept for about 2 hours then headed in to work on Monday morning. I was about an hour late for work and the entire office were absolutely amazed that a mere 10 hours earlier I had been swimming across the English Channel. I got a standing ovation - 1) for my effort and 2) for my madness to have done something like that and still come to work nearly on time.

In all honesty, the anti-climax was huge and I could not sleep properly for the next three days. I had to busy myself doing something otherwise I would have driven myself crazy. From a physical perspective, I was recovered by the end of Monday but the mental downer that I experienced lasted a lot longer.

The Aftermath

I was now lost. I busied myself at work and wrote personally to thank all the people that had donated to my charity, with an attached summation of the event. I also went to the charity's Christmas fundraiser. My supporters and I had raised about £5000 for the charity and they were immensely grateful and proud of me. It took a very long time to sink in that I had entered into a fairly elite group of people from all walks of life, some traveling across the globe to do this. I had met some amazing people along the way and to this day still keep in touch with many of them. To top it all off, my back problems were gone. I had achieved my goal. Yes, a bit of an eccentric way to sort out your back problems but you will never get to experience what it is like and I guarantee you will not meet such an inspirational group of people whilst sitting in a chiropractor's or osteopath's chair.

Over time I was slowly drifting back into my old patterns. I really did not want this to happen but without a goal in mind, I was going backwards and it was my friend Simon Grint, who had followed me throughout this Channel journey and may have been a bit envious, who came up with the Extreme Five as I mentioned earlier. Cycling, running, kayaking, golf and raising money. Luckily for me, Simon is great at organising things (something I am terrible at) so under his guidance, he, Mike Bass and I did this utterly bonkers challenge. It was awesome to have others on board to help. The three of us did all the events with others joining us for some of them. It was also very nice to have others to train with as I usually do most of my training on my own. The camaraderie and the friends made over these challenges were amazing. Amongst those friends there are some bloody amazing stories from the participants who take part in these events.

So 2009 was taken care of with regards to a goal and it took up a fair amount of my time and mental focus. With other pressures of life taking their toll, it was another few years before I managed to get a spot to swim Lake Zurich. It is one of the top swims out there so fills up quickly and it generally takes two- or three-years' worth of attempts to get in before you finally get a place. I had been out of training for about 2 years when I finally managed to get a place, so it was now time to get in the pool and follow the usual regime of base testing then move onwards from there. It was an opportunity to experiment a bit with my training a bit and focus more on the lakes than the ocean. For anyone who wants a great swim to do, look this one up. The lake itself is gorgeous, but I would suggest making a long weekend of it and exploring the surrounding area. This was then the start of a good few years of swimming and it is pretty much what I have stuck to entirely in the last five years.

My journey is now entering another chapter. In 2018, I was lucky enough to be on the very first open water swim coaching course that is held under the auspices of the STA. It has been rewritten by some pretty big names in the open water world - headed up by the English Olympian Keri-Anne Payne and put together in collaboration with some great swimmers from all areas of the sport. A curriculum was produced and in April 2018 I became a qualified open water coach. I then spent the season building up some credibility in this game, which all coincided with my ten year "Channelversary" (Channel anniversary); then there was only one thing for it. I needed to find a challenge that was equal in length or longer than the English Channel and take it on. One immediately sprang to mind. Lac Leman in Switzerland. A 69km swim down the entire length of the lake. Sadly, it was out of my price range, so I found the biennial Loch Lomond swim in Scotland. It is the same distance as the English Channel, but a fair bit colder and the entire swim is at night. This turned out to be a huge learning curve for me, and my hardest swim to date. I still have my sights on Lac Leman and possibly longer swims in my future. There are many accolades out there in the Open water world. However, I also have aspirations of inspiring others to take on their goals and achieve their dreams. The journey so far has been awesome and the people that I have met are amazing. It does not stop here; it is just time to take it in another direction.

If you had told me eleven years ago that I would be floating around different lakes and oceans around the world, taking on some of the biggest swims in the world, blogging about them or writing a book on my experiences and becoming a swimming coach, I would truly have laughed at you, and told you that the description fits someone extraordinary and definitely not me. But my original reaction still stands. Swimming channels and lakes is for mad people. Phenomenal, inspiring, tenacious – but still mad people! I am honoured to be included in such an amazing sport.

Epilogue

A journey is never without its ups and downs and through those up and downs there are a lot of people that are there to help you through it. This Journey is just that. Something that would never have been fathomable without the help and interjections of many people whom I would like to acknowledge

First and Foremost my family.

Pygmy Hippo AKA Spencer. The reason I went down this route

Brian and Mandy Schlachter who are the reason I am on this planet and have given their time love and support throughout many of my mad adventures.

Rachelle Schlachter who helped me through the initial trying times of getting into this game, by being there for me, acting as a sounding board when having to make the big decisions about the challenges I took on, and with development, organisation and implementation of the Extreme Five challenges and events. She was there with burgers and chips after my 6, 7 and 8 hour swims, and drove me back to London many times after my training sessions.

Then there are my great friends of which there are way too many to mention but a few who deserve a special mention as follows;

- Simon Grint and Mike Bass, and their respective partners who were instrumental in development of the Extreme Five challenges and in keeping my momentum in sport going and being absolutely amazing friends
- Nick and Lottie, who after having just arrived back from Boston drove down to Dover on Saturday night to see me off on Sunday morning across the Channel.
- Doug and Judy Robinson who were not only there at the start but saw me back at 3am on Monday morning, with champagne – in crystal glasses!
- Graham Williams for supporting us, lending us kayaks and helping us with Extreme Five
- Greg Wood – my training partner, buddy swimmer and great friend. (I still beat you!)
- Alison and Freda Streeter – for piloting my boat and putting up with all my crap on the beach and being there at 3am in the morning to share my success.

My larger Swimming group who are definitely too big a group to mention individually but who give me constant support and inspiration. A couple of people who deserve a mention and my thanks are Mark Sheridan, Dr Nicholas Murch, and Sydne Didier for their encouragement and advice.

My sponsors over the years who have helped me both financially and also by maintaining my website, specifically Colin Durrant from Okapi Computers who has been a massive help and Altered Images who continue to employ me and have helped out immensely over the years.

Whilst friends may come and go, there is one person who does not have a choice but to put up with me throughout all of this. Audra Schlachter – The Slimhippo. My loving wife who, single handed supports me and all my smaller swims, takes the time to teach herself to kayak and endures hypothermia along the way, puts up with a Hippo's grumpiness and generally does all the planning on my bigger swims.

The people who continue to inspire me, namely Lewis Pugh, United Nations Oceans Advocate who I've been fortunate enough to meet and have attended some his talks, Keri-Anne Payne, Olympic medallist and my open water swimming coach and mentor, and Jaimie Monahan, international marathon swimming hall of fame inductee and ice swimmer, and her partner Arik, some of the kindest inspiring people we know.

Thank you for taking the time to read this journal and I hope that you felt it useful and inspiring and help you to take on your own journey. If that happens to be in the water, then please keep in touch and keep following my blogs at www.zimhippo.co.uk

Now for the answer to the question about how hippos are able to spend so much time submersed in water.

Their leg bones have a very high bone density in comparison to human bones effectively making them weights to keep them submerged and on the bottom. Hippos are actually not good swimmers at all but rather walk/trot or gallop along the bottoms of lakes and rivers.

Printed in Great Britain
by Amazon

79739726R00133